W

Say Goodbye to Debt

Say Goodbye to Debt

KEITH TONDEUR

Marshall Pickering

An Imprint of HarperCollinsPublishers

Marshall Pickering is an Imprint of
HarperCollins*Religious*
Part of HarperCollins*Publishers*
77–85 Fulham Palace Road
Hammersmith, London W6 8JB

First published in Great Britain
in 1994 by Marshall Pickering

10 9 8 7 6 5 4 3 2 1

Copyright in this compilation © 1994 Keith Tondeur

Keith Tondeur asserts the moral right to
be identified as the author of this work

A catalogue record for this book is
available from the British Library

ISBN 0 551 02826-2

Printed and bound in Great Britain by
HarperCollinsManufacturing, Glasgow

Acknowledgements

I would like to thank various people and organizations without whom it would have been impossible to write this book.

First, I suspect that all debt counsellors rely heavily on the Child Poverty Action Group's yearly Benefits books, and also the *Debt Advice Handbook* by Mike Wolfe is invaluable.

Various friends and colleagues armed with red pens have helped both factually and in easing my rather cumbersome style! My thanks to Steve Lown, Len Mead, Alex Parry, Ian Roberts and Ruth Sands.

Special thanks go to Martyn Eden whose idea for a small booklet spawned this full size one, to Mick Wood of Harvesters Trust who provided virtually all the information for the chapters on court procedures, and to Liz Lown who diligently, accurately and speedily typed and re-typed cheerfully as deadlines approached and I became more fretful.

I would like to thank my wife Carole and our sons Luke and John for bearing with me as I locked myself away for hours at a time with only a coffee and Mars Bar for company – I promise I will try to be a better husband and father in future!

Lastly, I would like to thank you for reading this book as it means that you are acknowledging the problem you are facing. My real desire is that it will meet you at your point of need and help you begin to say 'goodbye to debt'.

Contents

Introduction

Why you need this book

Over the last few years a debt epidemic has taken place in this country and there are precious few signs of it going away. Nearly everyone will know of friends or members of their families who are experiencing it. You may even be in debt yourself. The vast majority will have been upright, law-abiding citizens who have got into difficulties through no fault of their own. An individual can do precious little if interest rates are doubled or if he or she is made redundant.

Suddenly they are facing an entirely new situation. Commitments taken on which appeared sensible when they had a steady income now seem crippling. Sources of credit which were recently encouraging extra borrowing are now demanding repayment. Many who had been in a steady job since completing their education have no idea how the Benefits system works. Neither have they been taught to handle money sensibly or been given basic budgeting skills whilst they were at school.

Is it any wonder then that debt leads to such panic? Panic can show itself in so many different ways. Some will go into a state of shock and adopt a 'head-in-the-sand, ostrich attitude'; post will remain unopened. Others will go to the other extreme – blaming everyone but themselves for the problem. In these circumstances other family members can find themselves on the wrong end of a verbal, or, sadly, sometimes even physical lashing out. Debt does not only affect the bank balance. It affects the balance of the mind and subsequent behaviour. Obsession with debt has even led to a number of suicides.

This is obviously deeply distressing and it is to avoid such tragedies that this book has been written. The stress of debt can be overcome. People can learn how to budget and how to fend off their creditors until they are in a better financial position. They do not have to keep their money hidden away. Debts certainly will not go away if they are hidden – and they won't stay hidden for long! By beginning to face the situation, you have already made a move which can only bring help and release. Reading this book because you recognize that you have a problem could be the first step, and certainly the biggest, on the way to saying 'Goodbye to Debt'.

If at this stage you are still wondering whether you need to read through this book I would ask you to spend a couple of minutes on the quiz below. It should soon clarify your situation!

How bad is your debt problem?

Quiz
1 Do you always pay your credit card bills on time?
2 Do you know exactly how much mortgage interest you are paying?
3 Do you know exactly how much interest you pay each month on credit cards?
4 Is your outstanding mortgage less than twice your basic income?
5 At current market value is your home worth more than you paid for it?

6 Do you know, without looking it up, the total of all your debts?

7 As a family, do you have fewer than two credit cards?

8 If you use store cards do you always pay off the balance in full each month?

9 Is it more than a year since you took on any new credit commitments (i.e. mortgage, bank loan, credit cards, etc.)?

10 Does the total of all your debts (including your outstanding mortgage) amount to less than twice your income?

11 Does your bank account pay interest when in credit?

12 Do you save money (excluding pension scheme)?

13 If you had a windfall of £5,000 would you be able to save it because you have no debts?

Every 'no' answer is a potential problem. If you answered 'no' to several questions you really could be drifting into debt without realizing it.

The aim of this book

It is quite clear that unemployment is going to remain high and that debt problems are not going to melt away. This book aims to be part of the process of doing something to alleviate the individual human misery debt causes. It will endeavour to do so in several ways. Firstly, it will give some detail on the economic background which has caused so many of the problems. By looking at these figures you will see that many people are in very difficult situations and realize that therefore you are not alone. Also it should help you to realize that if you are in debt it probably is not your fault!

Secondly, the book should help you come to terms with

your emotions. Many people facing the stress of debt and/ or unemployment think they are losing their sanity. In fact, what is happening to them is perfectly natural given the pressures they are under. By recognizing these pressures one should be able to channel them for good, rather than allowing them to fester and cause all kinds of adverse side-effects.

Thirdly, it shows that there are things that people in debt can do. They are not, as they often feel, powerless. There are practical steps they can take to start to rectify their situation. And for those who are just keeping their heads above water (and a recent survey indicated that this is a large number of us) this book should give sufficient guidance to prevent future problems by taking avoiding action now.

Lastly, the book aims to stop you feeling hopeless. Many will look at their debts compared with their surplus income (if any) and feel they face a lifetime of paying with absolutely no light at the end of the tunnel. Hopefully, when you have followed through the workings of this book much of this gloom will have lifted and an end to your financial problems will be in sight. It might not be very easy. It will, however, certainly be worth it.

What you can get out of the book

This book is going to be of use to different groups of people. Many of you may be reading it because you already have debt problems, in which case it should offer real help and support, and although a few parts may not apply to your specific situation it is likely that most will. As well as offering practical advice the book will provide sample letters to help you write to your creditors, as well as indicating which are the most important to pay first. If you are in this category it really is worth reading through the book before attempting to negotiate straightaway with creditors. It could save an awful lot of pain in the future.

If you fear debt may be closing in on you or your are worried about the future (i.e. you may fear unemployment or be expecting a baby) then various points will be of great use to you. These would include the chapters on budgeting as well as the practical money-saving suggestions. The chapter on the special problems of redundancy could also be of particular interest to you.

Lastly, you may well be trying to help someone else who has a debt problem – and if you are may I say thank you on their behalf. Someone who comes alongside offering both emotional and practical support can be invaluable. This book should help to give you a regular insight into their situation, a better understanding of their emotional pressures and some solid practical advice.

Whatever category you may find yourself in, my hope is that you will find this book useful. Almost on a daily basis I see cases where debt brings distress. This is usually caused by not facing up to reality, not knowing what to do or not knowing where to turn for help. By moving quickly, facing your emotions and taking practical steps the monster of debt can start shrinking before your eyes. I hope this book goes some way towards helping that process take place.

one

Some Facts About Debt

Economic background

Credit is not something that has just happened. In the earliest economies when bartering took place some form of crude credit agreement must have been made between the trading parties. But it was in the latter years of the last century when it developed, especially in the form of hire purchase for such things as bicycles and cars.

Since the Second World War the demand for personal credit has grown. This was precipitated by an ever-increasing percentage of people wanting to buy their own homes, as well as by what was perceived as an increasing 'need' for a considerable number of consumer durables.

During the 1970s there were dramatic increases in the price of oil. This meant that many Oil Producing Exporting Countries (OPEC) earned significant extra income – and much of that was invested in Britain. At first the banks used the money in the Third World but it became clear by the early 1980s that many of these countries would be unable to repay their loans. So the banks had to look elsewhere to invest their money, and with industry going through a downturn it was inevitable that the personal borrower became the target.

After the Conservative Government was elected in 1979 they started withdrawing the credit controls which had been imposed on the lending institutions, which resulted in a large surge of demand for personal credit, especially for mortgages. Credit became an industry. Money spent on advertising credit cards on television and in newspapers between 1980 and 1990 rose from £3.6m to £21m. Sums of money of this magnitude are only invested when a substantial return is expected.

The deregulation that took place in the 1980s helped encourage different financial institutions to explore new markets. Thus many banks started lending to customers for mortgages, and many building societies were granting loans for new cars and home improvements in the widest context of the words! It was a case of shop around. Credit had become fashionable, and financial institutions were falling over themselves to offer their customers an ever-increasing selection of services – including insurance, house purchase, share transactions, etc. Of course, many such services had no direct involvement with credit, but the point is that a customer attracted to a bank to obtain a loan may well for the sake of convenience go to the same bank to do his other financial transactions. So credit became a selling point. And as the range of services on offer increased, so credit became even more important as a means of attracting customers. Credit is also attractive for a retailer. Firstly, if they can persuade someone to open a store account they will almost certainly ensure that he will make further purchases from the store. Secondly, they will be getting an extremely useful customer profile completely free, which should enable them to enhance the effectiveness of their store layout and advertising. No wonder we are constantly bombarded with instant credit offers!

The final reason that personal credit became so freely available is because of technology. Instant credit, with immediate access to credit reference agencies, requires considerable sophistication. What is more, a central checking system enables immediate responses – particularly if you have received credit before. It is ironic, but the fact is that you are more likely to be accepted for credit if you are servicing satisfactorily a large amount of borrowing. The system of acquiring credit may seem inhuman, and that's because it is. Depending on your various answers to questions, your address, etc., points will be added up to see whether you pass the test. If you fail it is worth checking into. Computers do make mistakes – or it could be because of a problem with the person who lived at your address previously. Sadly, it is true that the poor and deprived, who probably need credit most to pay for essentials, will not get it in this way. Computers do make mistakes – but they don't have emotions.

Adding all the above together led to an explosion of credit. Between 1981 and 1993 the amount of personal consumer credit trebled, and if anything the increase in mortgage lending was even higher. As a result the percentage of personal lending by the banks had risen from 39% in 1980 to 57% in 1993 – an increase of almost half.

Some facts and figures (1992)

Amount of personal borrowing   £52.5 billion
(excluding mortgages)
This is equivalent to £2,300 per household

Number of houses repossessed
1989	14,000
1990	44,000
1991	75,000
1992	68,000

(But the number of repossessions has fallen only because of a change in building society policy which has brought about a huge jump in significant arrears cases. At the end of 1992 over 350,000 households were more than six months in arrears. Building societies used to repossess after three months.)

1.5 million homes are worth less than their mortgage.

Arrears

Electricity	70,000 disconnections. OFT estimate 1.5 million struggling to pay bills.
Gas	20,000 disconnections. OFT estimate 1 million struggling to pay bills.
Poll/Council Tax	This is very regional, but in certain inner city areas non-payment is in excess of 30%.

Approximately 30% of the interest rates charged by credit/store cards are indirectly due to other bad debts.

There are several million court summonses for debt each year.

The National Association of Citizens' Advice Bureaux (NACAB) now indicate that debt is the major area of request for help.

About half of all single parents are in debt.

The average debtor will have eight debts totalling more than £10,000.

Different sources of credit

1 Banks
These remain at the forefront of lending and accounted for some £34 billion of lending in 1990, a fourfold increase from ten years previously. To achieve this banks have

aggressively marketed consumer credit. During the period 1981–8 banks' advertising expenditure on financial services alone increased by virtually 250% in real terms. Not surprisingly this has changed the whole inner perception of the bank and particularly their relationship with the customer. Many bank employees at a senior level knew that their salaries and bonuses meant targets of lending had to be met. There was a time, therefore, particularly in the mid to late 1980s, when banks were keener to sell 'credit' than they were to encourage careful debt management. The weakness of this policy is reflected in the fact that the 'ideal' customer is someone who needs higher and higher levels of credit but who can always just manage to pay. Thus any change in circumstance such as redundancy or a rise in interest rates can quickly cause major casualties.

Certainly it can be argued that the extension of bank credit has helped many survive periods of hardship. However, there have also been far too many cases where families have been encouraged to take on too high levels of debt, particularly for non-essential items. This has created a false standard of living which is hard to do away with once people have got used to it.

Lastly, banks have tended to lend to people who fit certain criteria; people who pass the credit-worthy test. About 25% of people who apply to banks for loans are rejected, and normally these are the very people who need credit the most – for needs rather than wants. Thus those with low income or living in poor areas are left in many cases to the shady lenders who charge significantly higher, and sometimes criminally higher, rates of interest. Over 10 million adults in this country have no bank account and are thus denied access to the cheaper forms of credit.

2 Building societies

The number of mortgage loans increased during the 1980s from 6 million to 9 million as building societies, encouraged by government policy, relaxed their lending criteria and houses were seen as a good investment. The high interest rates of the early 1990s and rapidly increasing fears of redundancy soon put paid to that. However, the increased availability of mortgages had resulted in many taking on very heavy mortgages in the belief that both income and house prices would go on rising. Some were wrong on both counts. Those who took out 100% mortgages without some form of mortgage protection or insurance have suffered most.

It is important for the Government that the housing market stabilizes and that prices actually rise. Many buyers of recent years have mortgages higher than the current value of their house (called 'negative equity'). This is a stumbling block to an active housing market as well as a discouragement for people in this category to increase their consumer spending. Various attempts have recently been made to revive the housing market, with mixed results. Certainly there is no cheaper way of borrowing for the standard rate taxpayer with a £30,000 mortgage with tax relief. However, nearly 40% of people who apply to building societies for loans, many of whom who will have first gone to the banks, will be rejected.

3 Finance houses

These basically started to help finance hire purchase but have moved into other areas with much of their lending going to cars. Because of the relatively high risk of default, interest charges are inevitably higher.

4 *Credit cards*

As credit boomed throughout the last ten years and was seen as a major step towards a cashless society, so the number of cards in use has soared. There are well over 30 million cards in this country, the vast majority being Access or Visa. This compares with 2 million in Germany. When you apply for a card you are given a limit to which you can use it and you have a minimum to pay off (which is often only 5% of the existing balance) each month. For high earners and frequent users these limits were often increased to very high levels. By increasing limits and allowing only a minimum repayment they create a passive attitude to debt. Thus many people find it very easy to drift quickly into quite sizeable debt. With interest being charged on interest, debt is easy to get into and hard to get out of. Despite the sharp fall in base rate in 1992 the interest rates of credit cards have barely fallen. This is partly to cushion their increasing bad debt experience, but also to counter the problems of fraud – over 5,000 credit cards are stolen each day.

Credit cards are very handy to have in your wallet or purse – perhaps too handy. A recent survey in America indicated that people with cards tend to spend 34% more than those who don't have them. In an effort to counter the criticisms that credit cards have brought, banks are now encouraging the use of debit cards such as Switch which can only take out of your account money that is already there. This is, therefore, both helpful when budgeting and a questioning factor as to whether you really do need to purchase what you have in mind.

5 *Store cards*

These are sometimes run by the companies themselves as a financial offshoot or run independently through a finance company. There is a convenience factor but as the APR

(Annual Percentage Rate of Interest) is usually about 5–10% above that of a credit card, and as you may be tempted to keep using it, it is not a cheap option. Shop assistants may encourage you to use this form of payment if they feel you are unable to pay cash. In certain cases they may even be on commission to do so. Once they have got a sale it is irrelevant to them whether you can afford the item or not.

Remember too that it is pretty pointless going to a shop and buying something because it is the cheapest price quoted only to purchase the product through a store card whose APR could be 10% higher than others in the high street. Many 'bargains' are not what they seem. For instance, if you buy clothes priced at £50 but take several months to pay for them on a store card, the actual final cost may be £60 or even more.

6 Credit for those on low incomes

Those who have been rejected by the bank credit system have to turn elsewhere to have their needs met. Cheque handling companies and licensed moneylenders represent the 'just about respectable' aspect of this. However, given that a survey of licensed moneylenders in Birmingham a few years ago showed that unsecured credit carried an average APR of 525% you might well question this. Obviously people in such a situation are completely undermined and literally have to starve or work twenty-four hours a day to survive.

The unlicensed moneylenders are even worse. Preying on the weak and defenceless – the immigrant community, single mothers, the homeless – they know no shame. They will use every trick in the book, honest or dishonest, to get their money in. Taking people's giros as they leave the post office or the use of violence means nothing to them. The highest rate that I have heard of being charged is

400,000% on an annualized basis. In reality this would mean something like borrowing £20 on a Friday and having to repay £50 the next Monday.) No one should underestimate the harm caused to those involved – fear, hopelessness and ill health being common. These will be looked at in more detail later in the book.

Different rates of interest (a rough estimate)

		Base Rate
1	Banks/building societies	*+2 or 3% (less tax relief on mortgages up to £30,000)
2	Banks/building societies	
	i without tax relief but authorized +2–7%	
NB	ii unauthorized	*×3–6%
3	Finance houses	×2–3%
4	Credit cards	×2–4%
5	Store cards	×3–6%
6	Licensed moneylenders	up to 100%
7	Unlicensed moneylenders (loan sharks)	whatever they can get

*+ = current base rate plus figures shown
  × = current base rate multiplied by figures shown

The main problem areas

Undoubtedly the artificially high interest rates as the Government unsuccessfully battled to keep Britain in the Exchange Rate Mechanisms (ERM) had a detrimental effect on many in this country. Some could not pay the much higher figures then expected for mortgage lending, while others lost their jobs as companies cut back or even went under. Faced with these pressures many households tried to juggle their various commitments, with the result that debts occurred where no credit facility was available. It is clear that the main problem areas are as follows:

1 Rent

Latest figures indicate that around one million households have problems in this area – with about 20% of tenants having rent arrears. There is a big divergence nationally, with a few inner city areas having over 60% of people behind in their rent. It is obviously not politically, financially or socially responsible to evict these people *en masse*, especially as most would have to be rehoused by the same council!

2 Mortgage arrears

This has been a rapidly growing source of personal debt. In the 1980s many people took on expensive purchases, incurring large mortgage commitments. Housing costs should be at most around 30% of net income. If however they were 40% or more and then interest rates doubled, it is clear to see why so many found it impossible to keep up the payments. As house prices fell the incentive to keep paying enormous sums for a declining asset evaporated and there were sad cases of people just abandoning their homes. In an effort to avoid a major political storm, building societies have been doing all that they can to prevent repossession. As it costs on average around £15,000 to repossess a house, it is not an entirely philanthropic decision. The advantage is that it does keep families in their homes. The disadvantage is that arrears can become a large problem for more and more people, and a way of satisfactorily solving this has yet to be found.

3 Fuel bills

On the face of it fuel disconnections have been declining and this sounds like good news. Sadly, the main reason for this has been the introduction of prepayment meters. Whereas these can be a helpful way of prioritizing your needs it can also lead to the elderly or young mums having no heating in January. Generally speaking, however, despite the numbers struggling to pay their fuel bills the companies involved do operate a policy of concern.

4 Council/Poll Tax
It is too early to tell whether the Council Tax will avoid the pressure and adverse impact of the Poll Tax. Many people in debt owe money for this. Part of the reason may be that they feel because it was so unpopular they will get sympathy for not paying. More likely is the fact they just cannot afford it. Sadly, the politically motivated 'won't pay' have damaged the cause of the 'can't pay', sometimes with tragic results.

5 Credit arrears
Arrears on credit card or store card purchase are usually eventually pursued by a debt recovery agency. In practice these are usually not as refined as they sound. The way the collection of debt occurs varies. Often a company will sell its debts to a debt recovery agency en bloc – let's say at 70% of their total. The agency will only start making a profit when a figure higher than that is recovered, so it can easily be seen that there are temptations to use methods which border on harassment.

Occasionally people with debt are stigmatized as irresponsible at best, dishonest at worst. In virtually every case this is not true. Factors outside the individual's own control, such as interest rate policy and unemployment, are by far the biggest reasons for the problem. Some certainly have too many commitments, but have been encouraged by both government ('become a nation of home-owners') and lending institutions ('take the waiting out of wanting'). Most people are in debt for the simple reason that they have no resources.

ACTION PLAN

1 Recognize the different ways you can borrow and learn to see which are the most expensive.
2 Know that many of the factors causing your debt problems are out of your control.
3 Reassure yourself. Know that there are many people in similar situations to you – you are not alone!

two

Emotions

This chapter looks at how debt affects people – how it can plunge them into crisis and lead them into despair, guilt and loneliness – but it also shows how by taking positive action we can overcome these problems. Please don't ignore this chapter and go straight on to the practical steps, because it can offer real hope for your future.

Emotions are strange things. Certainly when debt strikes you may find that all sorts of different ones emerge. For this reason it is good to focus our attention at the beginning of this chapter on the actual causes of your problem. *You cannot blame yourself for something which happened totally outside of your control.*

Factors contributing to debt

1 Lack of financial education
One of the saddest things is that when the unexpected happens financially few of us know or are prepared for what to do next. We have probably remembered lots of things from our education, but cannot recall anything to do with handling money. This is because we were never taught about it in the first place! Most people in employment do not budget; they tend to live up to or just beyond their means thanks to the use of credit. Is it any wonder panic sets in when income suddenly falls or stops?

To most of us the Benefits Agency is equally confusing. People who have been working since leaving education have never needed to know how the system works. Is it surprising then that so many people do not claim the benefits to which they are entitled?

It is this lack of education that often gets us into trouble in the first place. We take on commitments which if we budgeted we would know we couldn't afford. We spend addictively, impulsively, we significantly underestimate our necessary outgoings and we do not make allowances for sudden adverse events like an interest rate rise or a belated tax bill.

Also because of our financial naïveté we have tended to believe what we are told. Most financial agreements are 'boring'. We don't bother with the small print often because we haven't understood the large! So we gladly sign away without working out the real long-term cost of what we are doing. Surely it should be compulsory to learn basic money management at school?

For a simple yet infallible budgeting method, see chapter 4.

2 *A sudden reduction in income*
There are many reasons for this, including:

- loss of job
- reduction in hours
- divorce
- illness
- business failure

The recession in the early 1990s was one of the longest and deepest on record. It took a great personal toll. There was a record number of company bankruptcies, and a great many companies had to cut staff and reduce hours for those who were left. Unemployment soared to above three million – well above 10% of the work force – and this undoubtedly has been the major recent cause of debt. *This is not your fault.*

3 Unexpected increase in needs

- a baby
- an unexpected bill, such as major house/car repairs
- an unexpected rise in interest rates leading to need to pay much higher mortgage/credit card commitments.

Again in this category the major recent cause of concern has been the large rise in interest rates. Although you were probably aware that interest rates could fluctuate, many would have been totally unprepared for a rise of approximately 50% in a relatively short period of time. People over the past decade have been encouraged to buy property rather than rent it, and even many council properties were sold. The experts led us to believe that house prices would continue to rise and the lenders encouraged us to borrow. Sadly many dreams have been cruelly broken in the last few years. Again *these are circumstances outside your control.*

4 Overspending and mounting credit commitments

Many of us continually overspend – indeed we are often encouraged to do so. Just think of the number of mail shots telling you how you *need* a loan and what a valued customer you would be. Remember as well how easy it is to be offered 'instant' credit from a whole variety of sources simply by walking down the high street. We only need to take on one too many of these commitments to be pushed over the edge, and then no amount of juggling will resolve the problem. A further problem is that if your circumstances change for the worse many of those who were keen to lend to you previously do a complete 'U-turn', worrying about their loan and often insisting they are repaid at a totally ridiculous rate.

5 An emotional crisis

Debt *rarely* strikes in isolation. It is often tied in with unemployment and can also be related to marriage breakdown. In a recent survey of couples who split up, money was named by over 70% as the number one cause of the problem. For example, if a partner leaves unexpectedly you will probably put all your energies into trying to resolve the problems, make sure any children are provided for and that you keep access to them. You have little time or energy at this stage for the bills that are piling up on the mantelpiece. Debt is creeping up on you but you are too emotionally taut to do anything about it.

It must be said that these factors do not automatically lead to debt. But whenever you take out credit you are making assumptions about future income which has not yet been received. And you may not get it! However prudently you borrow, circumstances can change quickly and unexpectedly and often lead to default. Debt has to be an inevitable consequence of an aggressive lending policy, and as such lenders will always expect to have to make some provision for bad debts to be written off. It is, therefore, right that we remember this as we come to look at our emotions – some of which, although being perfectly understandable, are irrational. Most of us will borrow because we are poorly paid, receive insufficient benefit rates or have been pressured to purchase things we do not have the cash for. We are forced into debt largely by factors totally out of our control, although we must not ignore the fact that our own personal desires can sometimes have a significant impact.

The need to be realistic with yourself

It is very tempting to push your problems away. After all, if thinking about them is going to depress you then maybe it's better to pretend they're not there. So you can put your head in the sand, refuse to open your post and if any creditor manages to make contact with you you can tell him that the cheque is on the way. Better still, why not carry on as if the crisis is not there at all and try and spend your way out of it? You could do with a holiday after all!

Or perhaps you feel hopeless and are just going through the routine of life. You no longer have either the strength or the will to do anything about your situation. You fail to respond to letters and phone calls, while the final demands pile up around you.

If either of these two pictures shows you as you feel – *you are in danger*. If you fail to recognize these warning signs you will very quickly find yourself in deep trouble. At this particular point in your life, pretending and doing nothing are the worst things you can do.

However, there are several things you can do right now to help you face your current situation:

1 Be realistic
The first thing you must do is face up to your situation, however hard this might be. It is hard enough to recognize that you may owe £1,000 on your mortgage repayments and £200 on a credit card – it is a lot harder, but also more realistic, to accept that you may have a total of several debts amounting to five figures or more. It sounds and looks horrible, but it is only by facing the full picture that you can begin to resolve your problem. Write out a complete list of your debts, large and small. **This is the first step back to financial health.**

It may be that you need to talk about it. Some of you will

know people you can trust and with whom you would feel at ease sharing your problems. Others may not feel confident enough to talk to anybody they know. In this case a visit to a Citizens' Advice Bureau or debt counsellor, or perhaps your family doctor, would be a good first step. Whichever route you choose, tell them about how you feel and why you find it so difficult to face the facts. Simply talking about it will take a great weight off your mind as well as giving you a better understanding of yourself. And remember the person you share with may well be able to offer real help and support, professionally and personally.

2 Act responsibly

It is important for you, your family and your future relationships with your creditors that you try to act responsibly at all times. This means first by not running away from the situation and secondly trying to resolve to honour your debts to the best of your ability. If, for example, your circumstances are just changing you should look for any areas where you could cut your spending so that you are still living within your means. However, if you are already experiencing financial difficulty you can take a first step by realizing that you are not powerless. You have legal rights and there are courses of action you can take which will make a real difference to your situation. I deal with this later, in chapters 4 and 5.

3 Take action

By doing nothing your situation can only get worse. You need to take action straight away. As you work through this book you should get a much clearer understanding of what your income is and what you spent it on.

However long you try to delay it the reality of your situation will hit home sooner or later. The longer you leave it the worse it will become, and at some stage it is possible that your position will go beyond the point of recall. In the vast majority of cases it is never too late, but remember – if you do nothing about your situation someone else may well do something which you would not welcome. It is far better to come to terms with it now while there are still many things that can be done to help.

Don't panic!

A recent survey (Gallup 1993) indicated that half this country's population is at best struggling to make ends meet. There has been an epidemic explosion of debt. Many will be caught in it. Over one-third of people questioned in one survey indicated that they couldn't sleep because of money worries. *You are not alone* – it's just that we are not very good at talking to each other about our problems.

Unfortunately, however, rumours and stories abound. You hear of bailiffs emptying your property of your possessions because you are a month behind on your credit card payments, or of a house being boarded up and the locks changed immediately you fall behind with your mortgage repayments. These sort of stories are not only untrue, they are very harmful and show the need for seeking expert advice rather than listening to ill-informed gossip.

However, when debt strikes your whole world can feel destroyed. In these circumstances it is the most natural thing in the world to hit the panic button and there could be a variety of causes that trigger this. You might suddenly have received a court summons because of unpaid bills or you may have just lost your job. It may be because you have just missed paying a bill on time for the very first time in your life, or it may be after you've missed six mortgage payments in a row. Debt collectors may have started ringing you or you may not be able to get into your home without the landlord continually demanding unpaid rent. Your gas might be disconnected or your washing machine repossessed. It could be one hundred and one things, but something will have hit home. Nearly each one of you will not have been in this situation before; you will not have experienced anything like it. You will probably be totally unprepared for what is happening and unsure as to where to go next.

Despite the fact that millions of people are in debt through no fault of their own, it remains a stigma. It leads to feelings of shame, guilt and loneliness, and because of the pressures it brings, perfectly normal people can do very abnormal things. Pride can be a real cause of inability to face facts. There are cases where people continue to 'go to work' on the same train every day for months after having in fact lost their job. Quite a few 'successful' executives will fight especially hard to keep their company car as part of their 'redundancy package'. Thus from outward appearances their neighbours will not know there is anything wrong. This effort to 'keep up appearances' can be disastrous. One well-respected businessman committed suicide the day before his house was due to be repossessed. This came as a total shock to all who knew him – including his family, who had no idea of any problems. We could surely prevent such tragedies if we were more honest with ourselves and those around us.

Panic leads to at least three patterns of behaviour which can only make matters worse:

1 Giving up hope

Debt and redundancy can easily destroy your self-worth. Just think of one of the first questions you use when you meet someone for the first time: 'What do you do?'

Followed shortly after by: 'Where do you live?' We have an unfortunate tendency to value each other materially and thus when we have lost our jobs or had nice houses repossessed these questions are devastating. One man who suddenly lost his job and fell into debt as a result said he felt like he had been 'kicked in the stomach'. Shock leads to a sense of despair. You feel you have been stripped of your dignity and you are tempted to lose hope.

2 Pretence
Others may try and overcome despair by pretending it isn't really happening. Perhaps they blame someone else. Perhaps they will convince themselves that a large cheque is due to them which will wipe away their problems at a stroke. So they change nothing and keep on spending at the same rate as before. Not only does this exacerbate the situation, but if they are hiding the problem from themselves they are also hiding it from their partners and friends who might otherwise be able to help. In one extreme case a family kept using new credit and store cards to try and pay off existing debts – by the time they came for help they had 88 cards between them!

3 Switching off
Many people caught up in a crisis of debt find it impossible to face up to those around them. After all they feel: 'I got myself into this mess and it is up to me to get myself out of it.' Thus their partners, children, family and friends are left completely in the dark as to what is going on and continue to live their lives as if nothing has changed.

If while reading this you feel you fit into one of these categories then please don't despair. Read on! These three destructive patterns of behaviour can be changed for something much better. The acute and desperately sad side effects of debt listed below normally only occur when people isolate themselves and fail to face up to their problems and do nothing about them. I'm putting these very depressing ideas here simply to warn you of what *could* happen. If you look at them as possibilities and then read on, they need never happen to you!

What not facing up to debt can lead to

The worries about long-term debt show themselves in many different ways. They not only have a detrimental impact on the person concerned but can have a devastating effect on those around you. It is so important to face up to the facts, to protect yourself and the ones you love, because constantly thinking about it can sap all your energy and bring you to breaking point. Here are some of the worst ways where untreated debt can strike:

1 Marriage breakdown
Debt puts a severe strain on relationships. Often one partner will feel guilty that he or she is in some way to blame. This will make him or her tense and moody. In many cases debt will go hand in hand with redundancy and therefore there is the added problem of lack of self-worth. In these depressed circumstances you may find yourself at home all day long, kicking your heels (and the cat) as you struggle to come to terms with what is happening. By being at home you could be disturbing your partner's routine, added to which it is unlikely that you will be very good company. In this situation it is hardly surprising that money worries are named as the number one cause of marriage break-up in over 70% of cases, as we saw earlier.

2 Child abuse

It is not only partners who suffer at times like this. Financial pressure will lead to stress at home and this can result in parents taking out their fears and frustrations on their children – especially if the children are making financial demands. The National Society for the Prevention of Cruelty to Children is only too well aware of this problem. In a major advertising campaign it carried a strapline: 'The worse thing about mortgage arrears is that children can end up paying.' Fortunately, not everyone in this situation resorts to violence but some do and just one is too many. But many children are shouted at or neglected because of their parents' money worries.

3 Health problems

It is becoming clear that debt is having a major impact in this area, with company welfare officers noting a marked increase in the number having to take time off work because of money worries. As they are probably fearful of losing their jobs as well this really is a catch-22 situation. Debt can lead to stress, shock and depression and this is particularly true in the case of older people. Many who lose their jobs or who see their standard of living drop sharply lose their self-esteem. They see it as a blow to their dignity.

4 Loss of friends

Because debt still carries a stigma it is not discussed and as a result friendships can be lost. Some friends will undoubtedly drift away, either because they feel debt is catching or because a friend in debt is no longer of any use to them. These sort of 'friends' you can well do without. However, your real friends are people you can talk to and share your problems with. Just because you can no longer afford to entertain as you used to or you are no longer able to buy your round of drinks, don't cut yourself off from them. True friends care for you and may well be able to offer all sort of help – practical, emotional and sometimes even financial. Don't be too proud to accept. They are offering help because they genuinely want to, not because they are looking for something in return.

5 Despair and suicide
It is important to recognize that a very small number of people have actually killed themselves because they allowed their debt problems to get out of control. In all the cases that I am aware of the person concerned had not felt able to share their problems with anyone else. Yes, debt can make the future look hopeless – businesses fail and houses are repossessed. It can look as if you will be in debt for the rest of your life. But there is hope and by reading this book you have taken the first step towards sorting things out. You have acknowledged that you have a problem.

So why is it so hard to face up to your emotions?

Barriers to facing the facts

Being unable to face the real situation is common – especially for men. Despite our changing society men still tend to see themselves as the breadwinner, the main financial supporter of the family. Therefore, when they fall into debt they often feel guilt, failure and shame very deeply indeed. They basically feel that it is their fault that they got into debt and they must somehow get out of it by their own efforts. It is precisely this 'macho' image that causes problems when it becomes apparent that they cannot cope alone.

There are several reasons why this may be so:

1 *Fear of having to tell your partner*
We will come on to communication in the next chapter, so suffice it to say here that it is likely that your partner will be more angry if he or she has not been told about the problem, than about your being in debt in the first place.

2 *Fear of any mistakes coming to light*
Everyone makes mistakes. Perhaps you had taken on too many credit commitments – they probably seemed all right at the time but now on a reduced income it is impossible to meet the payments. Perhaps you misunderstood the terms when you took on a credit agreement so you are repaying considerably more than you expected.

3 *Fear of someone saying 'I told you so'*
Perhaps you took out a loan to buy a new car which at the time seemed like an unnecessary extravagance to the rest of the family. Now you can't afford the repayments and will have to admit that they were right and you were wrong. This is never easy, but you will gain respect for your honesty.

4 *Fear of humiliation*
No one likes losing face and you may fear that this will happen to you. You may think that your creditors will automatically take you to court and that this will be reported in the local newspapers. You fear large vans with the words 'debt collector' written on the side parked outside your house for everyone to see. *This will not happen*. Creditors are not allowed to harass customers who are in arrears, and any court action will take place in private with no press around.

5 Fear of admitting there is a problem

One of the problems we have in this country is the British 'stiff upper lip'. When asked 'How are you?', we reply 'Fine', almost as if we are programmed to do so. In fact, we are so conditioned to hear that answer that if a different one emerges we almost certainly won't take it in. We are afraid to show our weaknesses, afraid to 'rock the boat'. So we try to carry on as though we have our world under control. It is possible to pretend that everything will be all right, but the longer we fail to admit the problem the worse it becomes. To retain the nautical metaphor, a shot across the bows will soon become a torpedo hitting amidships if no avoiding action is taken.

6 Fears that others will reject you

You may be afraid that others will not want to know you when your problems come to light. Genuine friends will, however, undoubtedly rally round. They may well provide the support and love that your family need at this time. They may also be grateful to you for having the courage to speak out so that they are able to share their fears and problems as well.

All of the above are strong fears and they are not easily dismissed. If any of them apply to you think through them and try to rationalize why you are feeling that way. Then start talking!

Acknowledging your emotions

Now that you have looked at the possible barriers that have been in the way you can begin to take some comfort from the fact that you are facing reality. Many people try to pretend that everything is all right and that they don't have feelings such as worry and fear. *These fears are perfectly normal.* You may have a combination of different feelings when you think about your debt problems. They may differ from creditor to creditor. Sometimes they will be directed outwardly and sometimes inwardly. Some of the most common emotions are fear, guilt, loneliness, anger, insecurity, powerlessness and hopelessness. There are many more. The bigger the problem, the deeper and more numerous will be the emotions. All these feelings show that you are doing your best to face up to what has happened.

It is important to recognize that you wouldn't be human if you didn't have feelings. Whatever you do you must take them seriously and make no attempt to squash them. They need to be worked through. It is also important to try and express them, otherwise you could become lonely and misunderstood. If you had a friend who was going through similar experiences it would be good to work through your emotions together. Knowing that someone else understands how you feel can be a great relief. If you are depressed don't hesitate to go and see your doctor. He will have seen many people with similar problems.

There is no quick and easy solution to many of the problems you have to face. In some cases hard facts have to be confronted. It is possible that you may never regain your former standard of living, and this is difficult to come to terms with as ours is a very materialistic society which places great emphasis on the status of wealth. But it is possible to change emphasis by putting family and friends ahead of material things. I can speak personally when I say that lowering your standard of living quite dramatically is difficult, but not impossible. My first marriage broke up partly as a result of working long hours to gain material possessions. In my present marriage I have less money but much more time with my wife and young children, and I can assure you I know which is better!

Helping family or friends in debt

If you would like to help a relative or friend who is in debt there is a great deal that you can do. It is firstly worth remembering that debt and unemployment cause emotions very akin to bereavement. So if you have never experienced the pain that your friend is going through just think how it felt when you lost someone close to you.

You could offer help in some of the following ways:

a Spend plenty of time listening to and working through your friend's fears and feelings. But remember, you are not there as a person who has all the answers, confidently handing down advice.

b Encourage your friend to talk about his thoughts and worries, especially relating to his health, family and friends.

c Try not to jump in with advice and instant solutions, and especially not criticism. Try to understand the other person so well that you are able to feel what it would be like in his shoes.

d Expect to be on the receiving end of some pretty strong emotions – such as fear, anger and guilt. Do all that you can to allow them to be expressed fully and naturally.

e Be aware that debt can spill over into all areas of family life. The pressure debt causes may well have led to some out-of-character incidents taking place. It is very important to try and talk these through so that they can be dealt with in an appropriate manner.

f If possible try and get all the decision-making members of the family involved in talking things through. This can be with you or not, depending on all the various circumstances.

g You might consider setting up a support group – a small number of friends who can be available to offer encouragement.

h Offer practical help. All sorts of things may have happened to your friend. He may have lost his company car; the bailiffs may have taken his lawn mower. Could you offer lifts to the unemployment office or the local supermarket? Could you lend your lawn mower or other tools he needs? Are you able to pay him for doing your gardening or decorating? Are you able to help restore his dignity by making him feel useful again? Perhaps you know of organizations who need volunteers and would very much appreciate his help.

i Try to make yourself available if new crises strike.

Debt brings a lot of negative emotions and this is quite normal. However, the sooner they are recognized and faced the easier it will be to control them. To do this effectively requires communication.

ACTION PLAN

1 **Face the full facts of your debt position.**
2 **Think calmly and positively about wanting to resolve the situation.**
3 **Acknowledge that debt causes pressure and stress which can lead to many mixed emotions. This is natural – and once you start facing up to your problems the pressure should start easing.**

three

Communication

One of the major problems with debt is that it is hard to face, and because of our lack of education in money matters we find it hard to communicate an accurate picture to ourselves, never mind anyone else! Later on in the book we will be looking at ways which will enable us to produce an accurate picture, but at this stage there is an urgent need to let everybody involved know that we are facing financial problems. *Debt cannot be handled alone.* You need all the love and support available from family and friends. You also need good advice from those who are qualified to give it. So take the plunge and start talking. You may find that a few of your fears will come to pass, but many others will simply vanish. What you will undoubtedly find is that you will get a great deal of support.

1 *Communicating* with your family

Above all make sure that you are open and honest with your partner and any children who are old enough to understand. Let them know the full situation. After all, they are not going to adjust their spending patterns if they are unaware of a need to do so.

It is important too to share with them how you feel about what has happened and to let them express their feelings as well. If, for example, you have kept your family in the dark for a long time it is very likely that you will be on the receiving end of considerable anger. Try to understand their feelings and give them time to allow the realization of what has happened to sink in. Be prepared for this to take time. In some cases your partner may feel so let down by your inability to speak out sooner that real pressures build up in your relationship. If this is the case you will both need time for reconciliation and this may be impossible to achieve without independent, expert help, so don't be afraid of speaking to a third party.

Remember that your partner is much more likely to be angry at your failure to speak out about the problem than at the problem itself. Experience shows that men have much more difficulty in this area – so speak out as the situations develop.

2 Communication with the Benefit Agency (DSS)

It is important that everyone regularly checks that they are receiving all the benefits to which they are entitled, and this is particularly true of those whose circumstances have changed, e.g. as a result of redundancy. Even government figures indicate that there are many people not claiming benefits to which they are entitled. It is a good idea to arrange an interview with a Benefits Adviser at your local Benefit Agency, and if you have been made redundant it is vital that you sign on immediately. But you may well be entitled to other benefits as well. It is sensible to ask what benefits you can claim. They will then have to go into detail to see what, if anything, you can receive. Obviously you need to explain your circumstances fully if you are to receive all the benefits to which you may be entitled.

A list of leaflets covering the different sorts of benefits is to be found at the end of the book (see Appendix 2). However, it is worth mentioning briefly here (see page 47) some of the major benefit entitlements (all facts correct at time of going to print):

CASE STUDY 1

Communicate With Your Partner

Margaret was worried. She was in partnership with her husband, although to all intents and purposes she was a sleeping partner. The last two or three times she had talked to him about his business he'd been extremely jumpy. But she reasoned that as he was away from home for so many hours during the week he must be very busy. Then she realized that no business letters at all had arrived at her home. She decided to ring the bank manager for an up-to-date financial position.

When she put the phone down Margaret was devastated. Her life had crumbled around her in minutes. The bank manager told her that he was about to ring her as his previous letters had gone unanswered. He was very sorry to tell her that he had no option but to appoint receivers. Furthermore, about three months previously her husband had instructed that all communications were to go through him at his business address. The reason soon became apparent. He had signed over their house as security for his business at that time. Even worse was to follow as it transpired that he had forged her signature on this and several other documents as well. By failing to communicate the husband had lost his home and his business — and even faced the probability of criminal action. Margaret too had lost everything. She felt destroyed by her husband's inability to talk through the problems with her — especially as she was in partnership with him.

Sadly, their relationship did not survive.

CASE STUDY 2

Communicate With Your Partner

Could it possibly get worse? Brian had been under
financial pressure for months. He had several credit
cards and a bank loan, and with a young family he
felt he needed them! But then he lost his overtime
and his income slumped. He looked for extra work
but couldn't find any. He tried to explain the
situation to his wife but couldn't find the right
words. She was only too well aware of the cost of
the food and clothes that she had to buy for the
children. Brian found he was reaching the upper
limit of his credit cards. In one case the limit was
increased, but in another he was warned that he
must start making some form of regular payment.
Just at his lowest ebb, Brian lost his job. How could
he begin to tell his wife? Something inside him
snapped. He got into his car and started driving. He
drove for three days, and when he finally came to
realize what he was doing he was at the other end
of the country. He spoke to a counsellor and
explained the situation. The counsellor rang Brian's
wife who was distraught and terrified that her
husband had killed himself. As far as she was
concerned the unemployment and debt problems
were secondary to the breakup of her family. But
even with this positive attitude much counselling
had to take place before they were able to feel
secure and trust each other completely.

SMART MOVE

Claiming Benefits

Mike and Tina bought their home with a 100% mortgage for £35,000. Their daughter was disabled and eventually became fully confined to a wheelchair. When interest rates rose they were unable to meet the higher payments and proceedings started when the arrears reached £200.

The building society knew that Mike earned £700 a month but didn't know that Tina had to stay at home at all times to look after their daughter, whose only income was the Severe Disability Allowance. As a result of finding this out they were able to strongly recommend claiming further allowances and it was found that their daughter was entitled to Disability Living Allowance and Tina was entitled to Attendance Allowance. The family's income increased substantially and they were able to resume full payments on the mortgage, thus ensuring their home was secure.

Means-tested and non-means-tested benefits

Some benefits are paid only if you have limited income and capital. These are known as means-tested because there is an investigation into your means before you can be paid them. Others are available to everyone who has made sufficient contribution to the National Insurance Fund, and in certain cases have passed residence conditions.

Of these non-means-tested benefits the most common are:

1 Unemployment Benefit

To obtain this you must claim at the Unemployment
Benefit Office. This is generally known as 'signing on'. It is
important that when you first claim you take your P45 from
your last job to the office. (A P45 details earnings, tax and
National Insurance.) You will not get any benefits until you
have signed on, so it is vital that you do this as soon as you
lose your job. You should not wait until you need the
money – sign on straight away!

Once you have made your first claim you will usually be
expected to make fortnightly visits to the office to sign on.
You will only receive the benefit if you have made enough
National Insurance contributions in the previous two years.
This is very complicated and shows the need for expert
advice.

Unemployment Benefit is not paid for the first three
days of unemployment, but thereafter it is available for up
to a year as long as you can demonstrate that you are
available for work and actively seeking employment. It is
always worthwhile keeping records of job applications to
prove that this is so.

After a year the payment of the benefit ceases and you
need to have worked for a minimum period of thirteen
weeks thereafter before you can reclaim.

2 Statutory sick pay and Sickness Benefit

Most people who are away from work due to ill health
receive statutory sick pay from their employers for the first
28 weeks. Those not entitled to this, but who are unable
to work receive Sickness Benefit from the Benefit Agency
for the first 28 weeks, provided they satisfy the contri-
butory conditions or have suffered an industrial injury.
After this period most people will be entitled to Invalidity
Benefit until either they can work again or they reach
retirement age.

The following means-tested benefits are also very common:

Income Support

This is the main benefit for people with a low income. However, it is not paid to people in full-time work who can claim family credit instead. If you are entitled to Income Support you also qualify for benefits such as free prescriptions and free school meals, council tax benefits and help with rent or mortgage interest costs.

You can claim Income Support if you meet the following criteria:

1 Your income is less than your applicable amount (this is the amount fixed by law which is meant to cover your day-to-day living expenses).
2 Your capital (ignoring home) is worth less than a certain amount (£8,000 in 1993).
3 Neither you or your partner are in full-time work.
4 You are not in full-time education.
5 You are signing on and actively seeking employment unless exempted from doing so.

You can claim for your family (you, your partner, any children) for whom you are responsible. In certain circumstances, where good cause can be shown, you can claim for up to one year in arrears. Unfortunately, lump-sum redundancy payments count towards your total capital and can, therefore, sometimes prevent Income Support being paid.

SMART MOVE 2

Income Support

Eighteen months ago Jane and Mark bought their £40,000 home with the help of a £28,000 repayment mortgage. Six months ago they jointly borrowed a further £8,000 from another building society to buy a car. Six weeks ago Mark left home, saying he would no longer be paying anything to the building society. Jane and her two children were left with only the Child Benefit and the small amount of maintenance Mark paid for the children.

Jane was told to apply to the DSS for Income Support straight away. However, with the mortgage already more than a month in arrears and with the DSS only paying half the interest payments for the first sixteen weeks, it was important to reassure the building society that things would stabilize after those sixteen weeks were up.

At first the DSS indicated that they would only help with the payments on the first mortgage because the further advance was not for necessary repairs or improvements. However, because of the breakdown of the relationship it reconsidered and agreed to pay the interest due on the car loan.

As the DSS would only pay interest the Building Society converted both loans to 'interest only' thus reducing the payments by £35 a month. The arrears of £600 which would build up in the sixteen weeks of half-payments were capitalized as soon as the first full interest payment was received from the DSS. Thus the arrears figure was maintained at a low level and Jane and her children bore no risk of losing their home, especially when the house was transferred fully into her name as part of the matrimonial settlement.

Family Credit

Family Credit is a tax-free benefit for low-paid workers with children and counts as a 'top-up' to your wages if you are in full-time work. You qualify if:

a Your capital is less than a certain amount (£8,000 in 1993).
b Your income is low enough – this depends on your circumstances and the number of children involved.
c You work in Britain at least 16 hours a week.
d You have at least one dependent child.

Family Credit is granted in periods of 26 weeks. This is good news if your situation improves, but obviously the reverse is also the case. After 26 weeks you will need to re-apply.

Housing Benefit

This is paid to people who have a low income and who rent their homes. It is paid regardless as to whether you are in full-time work or not and it can be paid in addition to Family Credit or Income Support. If you are a council tenant your rent account is credited with your benefit in the form of a rent rebate. If you are a private tenant you are paid a cash allowance.

You can claim Housing Benefit if:

a Your income is low enough – again this depends on various circumstances.
b Your savings and other capital are not worth more than a certain amount (£16,000 in 1993).
c You or your partner are liable to pay rent for accommodation.
d You normally occupy that accommodation as your home.

CASE STUDY 3

Check Your Benefits

Angela's husband was so happy when he got the job. He had been out of work for months and it gave him a real lift when he got the letter which told him he had a job. Sure enough the pay was bad, but his self-esteem was boosted just by working. Angela was very pleased for him and the last thing she wanted to do was destroy his fragile self-confidence. But the trouble was she just could not manage to provide for their two small children on the amount of money he was giving her.

Something had to give and Angela decided that after buying basic foodstuffs and other essentials for the family she could not afford the rent and so she stopped paying it. Every day Angela lived in fear of the landlord getting in touch, so every day she tried to ensure that she got to the post before her husband. The situation dominated her thinking. She was so preoccupied she was almost knocked down by a bus and eventually her doctor prescribed Valium.

One day the inevitable letter arrived. She was determined to do everything she could to protect her family, but by now the pressure had unhinged her thinking. She went to see her landlord and an hour later she had 'paid the bill' by sleeping with him.

In floods of tears Angela told her counsellor what had happened. She said she had not been able to look in the mirror since and she was very afraid that her husband would find out. The counsellor didn't know how to tell Angela that because of her husband's low income the family was entitled to benefits which would have covered the rent they needed to pay.

CASE STUDY 4

Check Your Benefits

It took a lot of courage for Julie to take expert advice. She had been brought up in a very strict and proper British family where you sort out your own mistakes. It was a very middle-class family where money and sex were two things that a respectable young lady should never talk about. But Julie was now at breaking point. As a result of a nervous illness she had lost her job some months before and the small amount of accumulated income had run out weeks ago.

Timidly she came for counselling and asked for help. The counsellor asked her a little bit about herself and then went through her monthly outgoings. He asked about her income and Julie reminded him that she wasn't working. He then asked which benefits she was claiming. Tears came into her eyes as she told him she wasn't claiming anything as she thought benefits were for poor people. Gently she was asked to empty her purse. There was nothing in it. It got worse. When asked when she had last eaten Julie informed the counsellor that a friend had given her a doughnut on Monday.

The interview took place on Thursday afternoon.

There is a large variety of benefits other than those listed above. For example, many sections of the community will be able to claim exemption from or a discount on the Council Tax. There is also a wide range of benefits for those with some form of disability. What you have just read is a very basic and simplified résumé of the benefits picture. This is all the more reason for checking out your own position at your local Benefits Agency, where you should be able to obtain a wide variety of leaflets covering all the different benefits. Alternatively you can obtain these leaflets free of charge from the DSS Information Division, Leaflet Unit, Block 4, Government Buildings, Honeypot Lane, Stanmore, Middlesex HA7 1AY.

Before leaving benefits mention should be made of the Social Fund. This was introduced in 1986 and was meant to establish for the first time a state credit system to replace the previous use of single-payment welfare grants which had been available to the unemployed and poor for the purchase of essential items. No interest is charged on these loans and repayments are to be made through the automatic deduction by the state of instalments due from the benefit check payable. Loans are limited to a maximum of £1000 and must be repaid within two years. If you are in dire need then seriously consider applying.

Communication with the tax man

This is another important area of communication. The normal method of tax payment (Pay As You Earn) is based on the tax year and makes assumptions about your annual income. If you lose your job or have your hours cut these assumptions are no longer true. It is, therefore, worth writing immediately to let them know if these circumstances apply to you. Your tax situation should be sorted out in due course but it could prove very handy to get a rebate earlier than otherwise might happen and when you could well need it the most.

Communication with creditors

If you are getting into financial difficulties you have a choice of what to do next. You can either ignore the problem, do absolutely nothing and just hope that your creditors don't notice that you have stopped paying your bills. It is so tempting to take this choice and simply hope that your money problems will disappear. But this will just not happen! You will start to get letters from your bank, building society or landlord. By not replying you will only make them more irate and far less likely to compromise in an effort to understand your situation. You could end up in court. You will certainly end up in a mess.

Alternatively, you have the option of letting your creditors know straight away that you are having difficulties making the repayments. By informing them as soon as possible you will avoid much distress, save time and usually receive sympathetic understanding. They can see that you are being honest, are wanting to tackle the problems and are trying to plan ahead as well as you can. The earlier you can do this the better, and it is well worth writing to them even if you see a potentially dangerous cloud on the horizon which eventually blows away.

For example, you may fear that there are going to be some compulsory redundancies at your place of employment. You obviously hope that you are not going to be one of them, but it is good to take precautions just in case you are. In this sort of situation it is worth spending some time making a list of all the commitments you might struggle to meet if the worst comes to pass and then write to them as soon as possible along the following lines:

Date   Your address

Creditor's name and address

Dear Sir or Madam,
    I am writing to inform you that it looks likely that there are going to be some compulsory redundancies at my place of work. I have to warn you that if I am

made redundant I will experience considerable difficulty in paying my mortgage/rent/gas/electricity/ Council Tax etc.* It is unlikely, given the current economic climate, that I will obtain another job straight away, although I can assure you I will be doing everything in my power to do so.

I am currently preparing my financial statement and will forward it to you as soon as it is ready. In the meantime if you have any suggestions that might help me meet my commitments to you more easily I would be delighted to hear them.

Obviously, if I do not lose my job I will continue to meet the payments to the best of my ability.

Thank you for your help.

Yours faithfully

(your name)

*Complete as appropriate

Remember, creditors are aware of what is happening to the economy. They know when recession or redundancy strikes. They will understand the financial pressures that sickness or divorce can bring. By keeping in touch and explaining your situation you stand a good chance of getting a helpful response.

The following quote from the Council of Mortgage Lenders' guidelines entitled 'Handling of Mortgage Arrears' shows that this is so:

When a borrower falls into arrears through no fault of his or her own, the problem is handled both sympathetically and positively. This requires that the borrower co-operates with the lender, in particular by reacting to correspondence.

The key point in dealing successfully with arrears problems is that the borrower should make contact with the lender (or vice versa) at the earliest possible time. The borrower is likely to anticipate problems before the lender becomes aware of them. Lenders want borrowers to contact them before arrears begin to build up.

Communication with advisers

Very few of us have received more than a basic financial education. It makes a lot of sense therefore to seek advice as soon as danger looms. Be careful where you go. Friends may know no more than you do and some of their scare stories, which are probably totally unfounded, will not actually help. Some debt counselling agencies who advertise their services charge for doing so. Others pretend to be debt counsellors but are really more like debt collectors. If in doubt – stay away. There are still places where you can get professional advice free of charge although they are under immense pressure. Citizens' Advice Bureaux and Money Advice Centres are the most common. If you do decide to go make sure you take all the necessary documents with you. Tell the adviser the position as clearly and quickly as possible. Be totally honest and do everything you are advised. This book should help you follow the process as it contains several form letters, sample budgets and lists of priority debts.

Remember that taking professional money advice will almost certainly help your financial position. It should enable you to maximize your income, reduce interest levels and re-schedule payments. It should also prevent you receiving any undue harassment from creditors and should help prevent eviction and disconnection of water, heat and light. Many of you will also avoid having to go to court if you follow the advice given in this book. And there could be significant long-term advantages as well.

Knowing you are following good advice should improve both your physical and emotional well-being. As hope and

CASE STUDY 3

Seek Advice

Michael was the director of a successful company, but then recession struck. In a desperate effort to save his company he took out a loan for £30,000 and gave a personal guarantee to cover it. It was to no avail. The loan did not save the company and he was called upon to repay it. In 1986 he took on a teaching job and endeavoured to start paying off the loan. He was asked to pay £150 per month and he did this without taking advice, even though it was threatening to push him into debt elsewhere.

You would think that Michael would struggle for years, but would eventually manage to pay the debt off. But even this was not true because the creditor insisted on charging interest. By the end of 1990 the debt, originally £30,000, had actually risen to £44,000. On the edge of despair and ruin Michael's marriage started to fall apart and it was only at this stage that he sought advice. Fortunately a stern letter, warning the creditor that in the current circumstances he was unlikely to receive any more payments, brought results. The creditor cancelled all interest thus reducing the debt significantly. He also cancelled half the resulting debt.

For the first time Michael could see light at the end of the tunnel. As a result he continued to make payments and has virtually got himself out of a horrendous situation as well as keeping family and home together.

confidence improve marriages can be saved and even suicides prevented. There should be a feeling of relief that your problem is being shared and a lessening of stress as well. This does not mean your difficulties are going to disappear instantly. Recovery is often a long and arduous process, but at least you know there is help at hand when the unexpected comes along.

ACTION PLAN

1 Talk openly about your debt problems to all members of your family old enough to understand.
2 Check with the Benefits Agency as to whether you have any unclaimed entitlements.
3 Write a letter to your creditors indicating actual/ potential problem areas.
4 Seek advice from experts.

four

The First Practical Steps

It is important that you take a deep breath as you start your practical moves to lessen your debt problem. People's natural inclinations vary. It is, therefore, important right at the beginning to prepare a plan which you must then try to keep to. It can be varied slightly to suit individual requirements, i.e. you may have to take avoiding action immediately if you are being threatened with a court summons, but listed below is a good strategy to follow:

Stage one – investigate

The first thing that needs to be done is to identify those areas where you have, or could potentially have, some debt problems. If you have existing debts but are managing to balance the rest of your income and expenditure it is simply a question of listing what you owe and to whom and then adding it up. It is always important to do this as it enables you to look at your total debt picture and compare it with your budget situation as well as any assets you may have such as equity in your house (that is, its market value less outstanding mortgage).

If on the other hand you have just lost your job, you have to think which areas in the future might cause you problems. In this case it is better to be on the safe side and write to as many potential creditors as you can think of.

Whichever category you fit into, you need to write a letter to your creditors along the following lines:

Date   Your address

Creditor's name and address

Dear Sir or Madam,

Re: Account number (enter your account number here – you can find this on previous bills)

Over the past few weeks I have been finding it impossible to balance my family budget (*or* I have recently been made redundant and very much fear it will be impossible to balance the family budget). As a result of this situation I have been getting financial advice.

To enable me to get as accurate a position as possible I would be really grateful if you could send me the following information:

1 The current position of my account.
2 What, if any, interest is being added to it on a monthly basis.
3 The date by which you expect me to have this account up-to-date.
4 The options open to me, given the above circumstances.

Once I have received the relevant information I will produce my financial statement and write again with my proposals.

Thank you for your attention.

Yours faithfully

(your name)

It is important to write to your creditors at this stage because it will help both them and you to get a clearer picture of your actual situation. They will be brought up to date with your current financial position and will also be aware that you have actually been seeking professional financial advice, which can only be a good thing. You will receive an accurate, up-to-date picture of the amount you owe, as well as discovering exactly what interest you are being charged on a monthly basis. At this stage there is no need to send a copy of your financial statement, because you cannot complete it accurately until you have replies from all your creditors.

If you have a mortgage it is important to write to your lender immediately. You need to inform them of your situation, but you need some additional information from them. You need to know that you have been paying the correct interest charge and that any MIRAS (Mortgage Interest Relief taxed At Source) has been properly worked out. It is also important to know the total owing, and you therefore need to ask for a redemption figure (the figure you would have to pay to clear the mortgage).

The letter you write to your mortgage lender should be along the following lines:

Date   Your address

Their address

Dear Sir,

Re: (enter your account number here – this can be found on your previous statement)

Over the past few weeks it has become impossible for me to balance the family budget. As a result I have been taking financial advice.

Would you, therefore, please send me the following information as soon as possible:

1 My present monthly payment.
2 The current interest rate you are charging.
3 Details of any arrears.
4 The redemption figure, including details of any charges you may make should I see this as an option.

I would also very much appreciate it if you could check that I have been paying the right interest rate and that you have calculated MIRAS correctly. If you feel there are any other suggestions you could make which would help me in my current situation, I would be very grateful.

I will be in touch with you again when I have received your reply and am able to put together my financial statement.

Yours faithfully
(your name)

If you have not already done so, now is the time to start keeping a file of all correspondence. It is vitally important to keep a copy of all letters you send as well as all those you receive. This should help to avoid any dispute or confusion, and if any court action is eventually sought by one of your creditors it could prove to be very useful evidence in justifying your position.

At this stage there may well be another letter that you need to write. Endowment mortgages were very fashionable throughout the 1980s (perhaps because the insurance salesman got very good commission on them!) and they are now very common. What happens is that you invest an extra sum each month which should mean that at the end of the mortgage term you are left with a tidy sum which will pay off your mortgage and hopefully leave you with a little nest-egg as well. In some cases this has worked, but because of an over-generous payment of terminal bonuses in the late 1980s the investment is not looking so attractive now, and there is in exceptional cases the danger that the lump sum received at the end will not even pay off the mortgage. Paying these fairly high monthly premiums is obviously exceptionally difficult if you are in debt. One of the other problems with this sort of policy is that it is very much geared to greater returns the longer it has been running. Therefore, if you tried to cash in an endowment policy to which you might have been paying £50 a month for two years you could well discover it is almost worthless.

If you have an endowment policy it is worth writing the following letter:

Date   Your address

Their address

Dear Sir,

Re: (enter your policy number here – this can be found on your previous statement)

Because of my current financial position I would be grateful if you could update me with the following information:

1 Confirmation of monthly payment figure and when the policy is finally redeemable.
2 The current surrender value.
3 The current paid-up value.

Once you have supplied me with these figures I will consider my options and decide whether I need to contact you again.
    Thank you for your help.
    Yours faithfully
    (your name)

A couple of the terms used in the above letter may be confusing. The 'current surrender value' is what, if anything, the insurance company would pay you straight away if you cancelled the policy. The 'paid-up' value is what you would be paid at the end of the term of the policy if you did not make any more payments. These figures can be very helpful in working out your various options, as it may well be that if your policy has been running for quite some time there is potential both to release cash and to reduce your payments. Your mortgage company may, for example, allow you to switch to basic life cover only, which would be much cheaper than an endowment policy.

At the end of the mortgage term you would still be owing some capital to the mortgage company, so this line of action does need careful thinking about. This would be a good avenue to explore, for example, if money was currently tight but you were expecting some form of inheritance or lump sum pension pay-out shortly. An increasing number of people have for one reason or another decided to stop their endowment policies recently, and as a result several brokers have actually started trading in these types of policies. So if you do decide to surrender your policy it is well worth checking with one of them before merely returning it to your insurance company. In some cases the policy could be worth as much as 30% more. The financial section of the more heavyweight press frequently carry details of their services.

As soon as you have written all relevant letters, and before receiving their replies, it is important that you start drawing up your budget. If you have never done this before it sounds daunting and to begin with it certainly involves much hard work. However, once it is completed and up and running it is relatively easy to keep up to date. It will provide a very useful pointer to you, particularly on where you spend your money. You might well be able to make some savings straight away as you realize just how much you are spending on items such as newspapers or chocolate!

Preparing your financial statement

Budgeting is the art of keeping your spending under control. Like many things it sounds simple in theory, but can be really difficult in practice. How do you start to live within your means? Whether you currently have a debt problem or not the quicker this can be done the better the situation will be, and you should start to feel greatly encouraged as you see your debts begin to decrease.

As budgeting has to be accurate to be effective you need to keep track of everything. When you go shopping keep all the receipts and record where your money went as soon as you get home. Remember that odd visits to the pub, the sandwich shop and the office vending machine add up. You may well find that you are spending far more in these sorts of areas than you think you are. The simplest way to record all this expenditure is to keep a pocket-sized notebook with you so that you can record everything at the time you actually spend it. If in conjunction with this you accurately record on your cheque stubs what you have paid out, you should build up a very accurate account of your finances.

At this stage some of you may look at what is involved in budgeting and think it is just not worthwhile. You may think you have a very accurate picture of what you spend your money on. Without wanting to disillusion you I would like to put this confidence to the test! Why not write down on a piece of paper what you think you or your family would spend on Christmas. Try and write down a figure straight away. Once you have done this look at the box on Christmas Spending and write in figures for each category. Then add up the total and compare it to the figure you had previously written down. If they are very similar you are either knowledgeable, lucky or dishonest! Incidentally, if anyone put down a figure of over £3,000 perhaps I could have a party invitation!

Christmas Spending

Presents	£
Cards	£
Postage	£
Decorations	£
Food	£
Drink	£
Fuel	£
Travel	£
Outgoings	£
Telephone	£
Other	£

CHRISTMAS SPENDING
Total   £

Seriously though, it really is important that we compare these two figures. You see, as such there is no right or wrong answer to the question. But the outcome could be highly significant. If, for example, you thought you would spend £700 on Christmas, but when you added it up the total only came to £600 everything would be fine. You would actually have £100 left over. However, if you wrote down a figure of £500 and it added up to £1500 you would have got yourself into debt to the tune of £1000. And it is in these circumstances that you can almost guarantee that heavy gas and electricity bills would arrive at the same time.

Hopefully this exercise will have convinced nearly everyone that there are several good reasons why you need to produce a budget:

• It will give you an accurate picture of your money situation.

- It could well enable you to reduce your spending and thus improve your overall position.
- It can be shown to creditors in an effort to convince them that your offer to them is fair and that you could not pay them any more.

Later on in this chapter you will attempt a fictional exercise to ensure you have got the hang of budgeting. Before you start to do this, however, it is important that you remember a number of key things:

1 **Be absolutely honest.** If you overstate your income or underestimate your expenditure (either by taking short cuts or missing things out because you think they aren't worth writing down) the only person you will fool is yourself. On this basis you may well make an offer to a creditor which is accepted that in reality you have no chance of paying. This will only infuriate the creditor, who may well give you no further chances of negotiation. So to prevent yourself getting into even deeper water do make sure the budget is as accurate as you can make it.

2 **Explore every option** that is available, either to increase income or reduce expenditure. This can be very difficult and may only make a marginal degree of difference to your actual position, but if a creditor sees you are doing this it is likely to influence his view of you considerably.

3 **Involve all family members** who are old enough to understand. If other members of the family are consulted they are much more likely to help and work together to make the operation successful. It is important too to remember that although there are family priorities there are individual priorities as well. Try not to criticize each other too much, but end up with a budget that all your family are happy to try and stick to.

4 **Keep your spending disciplined**. Your budget will soon be shot full of holes if you do not use it to guide your spending. Stick to the shopping lists you produce and try to cut out all impulse spending. Even 'small' items like magazines – perhaps a woman's monthly, a couple of sports or car glossies – can add up to £5 or more a time. If this £5 occurs each week, that's £20 a month or £240 a year.

5 **Pay by instalments** whenever you can. Most things such as gas, electricity, TV licence, Council Tax, etc., that you are supposed to pay quarterly or annually, can now be paid on a monthly basis. It really is a good idea to do this wherever possible as it enables a more accurate picture to be built up on a month-by-month basis. It should also help reduce the number of unexpected or forgotten payments you will have to make.

6 **Look at your statement carefully**. When you have finished go over it once more. Can anybody think of anything that is missing?

Now that you have got the necessary principles you need to start putting them into practice. The first thing to do is to add up all your *income*. Try to include everything here, including anything that your partner earns as well as any benefits you receive. It is best to ignore bonuses and overtime unless they are guaranteed, because if you include them and spend to the full you could quickly find yourself in debt should they disappear.

Once you have calculated your income you have to turn to your outgoings and in essence you have to produce a list of everything your family spends money on in the course of the year. The first and largest area is your *formal commitments*. These include a variety of services you have to pay for on a monthly, quarterly or annual basis. Your mortgage/rent comes into this category, as do your electricity and gas bills, Council Tax, car insurance and road tax. There are many more and pages 76–7 list them for you in some detail. Remember to multiply all weekly payments by four and divide all quarterly ones by three. Annual payments are divided by twelve. By doing this you are ensuring all costs are looked at on a like for like basis, i.e. monthly, especially if that is how you are paid.

After you have completed your formal commitments you need to look at your *everyday spending*. This is basically your food and grocery shopping, but also includes milk, newspapers, sweets, etc. By the way, one of the first things you need to do when budgeting is to acknowledge the difference between a 'need' and a 'want', between an essential and a luxury. At the risk of alienating every reader it might look something like this:

Essentials	**Luxuries**
Mortgage/Rent	Telephone
Water Rates	TV Licence
Ground Rent	Car MOT
Council Tax	Road Tax
Property Insurance	Car Insurance
Contents Insurance	Personal Insurance
Electricity	School Fees
Gas	Toys and Books
Oil/Coal	Petrol
Maintenance	Parking
Basic Foodstuffs	TV Rental
Laundry/Dry Cleaning	Video Rental
Chemist	Records
Public Transport	Hobbies
Essential Clothing	Newspapers
Dentist	Alcohol

Essentials   **Luxuries**
Optician   Tobacco
Essential Repairs   Redecoration
                       Trips Out
                       Meals Out

This list should not be treated as 'correct'. Every individual will have different priorities, and for some people items such as telephone, car, television could appear in the first category. It is important too to remember to try and keep a little left over for some hobby or other form of escape.

Lastly, you need to remember your occasional costs. These are largish items of expenditure that either come up at certain times of the year, like birthdays and Christmas, or else crop up unexpectedly, such as car repairs or decorating.

To help you get the hang of it I have produced a fictional example which you should try and sit down and resolve in your family group:

Mr and Mrs Peabody live in a modern semi-detached house in a suburban area and they have a net income of £1,000 a month. They have two children, Sally aged 14 and John aged 7. Mr Peabody likes a drink and has to travel into the city to work. His wife, a heavy smoker, stays at home. Sally is into the latest fashion, while John is just getting into computers and likes taking Tiddles, their Alsatian, for walks.

Now look at the Budget Form for the Peabody Family. To give you a start some information has been filled in. How do you think they would spend the rest of their income? Remember – you cannot spend more than your income.

The Peabody Family Budget

MONTHLY INCOME   £1,000

DETAILS OF MONTHLY EXPENDITURE

1 Formal Commitments

Mortgage	£	350
Council Tax	£	45
Electricity	£	50
Water Rates	£	20
Telephone	£	30
TV Licence	£	7
Car: MOT, Tax, Insurance	£	20
Credit Repayments	£	
Household Insurance	£	
Formal Commitments – Total 1	£	

2 Everyday Spending

Food	£
Sundries	£
Baby Maintenance	£
Children's Pocket Money	£
Childminder	£
School Lunches	£
Toys and Books	£
Pet Food	£
Laundry/Dry Cleaning	£
Chemist	£

Petrol   £
Parking   £
Public Transport   £
_____

TV Rental   £
Video Rental   £
Evening Classes   £
Sports/Hobbies   £
Records and Tapes   £
_____

Alcoholic Drinks   £
Cigarettes/Tobacco   £
Newspapers/Magazines   £
Other   £
_____

Everyday Items – Total 2   £
_____

3 Occasional Costs
Christmas   £
Birthdays   £
Holidays   £
_____

Car Repairs   £
House Repairs   £
Redecoration   £
Vet Bills   £
_____

Clothing   £
School Trips   £
Dentist   £
Optician   £
Meals Out   £
Other   £
_____

Occasional Costs – Total 3   £
_____

TOTAL MONTHLY EXPENDITURE

Total 1:	£
Total 2:	£
Total 3:	£

Grand Total:	£

Balance

Monthly Income:	£1,000
Monthly Expenditure:	£
Monthly Surplus:	£

How did you find that? It is not as easy as it looks, is it? Many of your may have found you had quite heated discussions with other members of your family regarding the Peabody priorities. Hopefully, you managed to produce at least a balanced budget. Well, now it's your turn.

Again as a family unit, and using all the information you have received from your creditors, your notebooks and bank statements, work out your own budget as accurately as possible. Remember not to include any payments you are currently making on existing debts. Apart from some of your occasional costs which can be very irregular and impossible to quantify 100% accurately, you should have a budget that is very close to reality.

Your Personal Budget

DETAILS OF MONTHLY INCOME

Your Basic Salary	Child Benefit
Spouse's Basic Salary	Income Support
Guaranteed Overtime	Family Credit
(Flexible Overtime)*	Other Benefits
(Flexible Bonuses)*	Maintenance
Pension	Disability Benefits
Other Income	

Subtotal £ _____   TOTAL INCOME £ _____

*Put in brackets but do not add to total as these figures cannot be relied on week after week. When they occur use to pay off debts or save as appropriate.

DETAILS OF MONTHLY EXPENDITURE

1 Formal Commitments

Mortgage	£
Rent	£
Water Rates	£
Ground Rent	£

Service Charge	£
Council Tax	£
Property Insurance	£
Home Contents Insurance	£

Electricity	£
Gas	£
Oil	£
Coal	£
Telephone	£
TV Licence	£

Car MOT £
Road Tax £
Vehicle Insurance £

Regular Saving £
Personal Insurance £
Private Pension £
Maintenance Payments £
Regular Giving £

Second Mortgage £
Loan Repayments £
HP Repayments £
Credit Card Repayments £
School Fees £
Other £

Formal Commitments – Total 1 £

2 Everyday Spending

Food £
Sundries £

Baby Maintenance £
Children's Pocket Money £
Childminder £
Toys and Books £

Pet Food £
Laundry/Dry Cleaning £
Chemist £
Petrol £
Parking £
Public Transport £

TV Rental	£
Video Rental	£
Evening Classes	£
Sports/Hobbies	£
Records and Tapes	£

Alcoholic Drinks	£
Cigarettes/Tobacco	£
Newspapers/Magazines	£
Other	£

Everyday Spending – Total 2   £

3 Occasional Costs

Christmas	£
Birthdays	£
Holidays	£
Subscriptions	£

Car Repairs	£
House Repairs	£
Redecoration	£
Replacement Furniture	£

Vet Bills	£
Clothing	£
Dentist	£
Optician	£
Trips and Outings	£
Meals Out	£
Other	£

Occasional Costs – Total 3   £

TOTAL MONTHLY EXPENDITURE

Total 1:	£
Total 2:	£
Total 3:	£

Grand Total:	£

Balance

Monthly Income:	£
Monthly Expenditure:	£
Monthly Surplus:	£

How does it look? At this stage you will really be hoping that there will be some surplus, however small, to help you start repaying your debts. But even if that is not the case, all is not lost. For example, you are now in a position where, with your budget completed, you can send a letter to your creditors which fully explains your situation. If you have no surplus you can ask for breathing space while you try and improve your situation. We will be looking into this in more detail later.

It is important to remember at this stage that even if you don't like what you see and you think your creditors won't either then it is still important to keep them informed. They may be rude or unhelpful, but they will be far more so if you fail to make and keep contact.

At this stage too it is worth keeping a list of all your creditors and what you owe them (and also of debtors if anybody happens to owe you money). Remember to amend this as you receive replies from your creditors, and show payments made and interest charged. It is important here to look at the various types of interest you can be charged because this will help your future strategy. The major types of credit are listed below:

1 **Secured**. This does not mean that you have got a good secure loan! What it does mean is that when you borrowed the creditor insisted on having some form of security from you before he agreed to lend you the money. So, in effect, if you fall behind in the repayments and all else fails the item that you agreed to secure on the loan, usually a house or insurance policy, can be claimed by the creditor. A good example of this is a mortgage.

2 **Unsecured** credit generally means that the lender has confidence in your ability to repay the loan and will in any case have built into the interest rate charge an allowance for the fact that you might default. Purchasing a fridge-freezer on hire purchase is a good example of unsecured credit.

3 **Fixed term credit** means that you pay back a sum of money each month for an agreed period of time. The amount of money may fluctuate as interest rates go up and down, but at the end of the period the debt will have been cleared. A bank loan, rather than overdraft, is an example here.

4 **Revolving credit** means that you only have to repay a minimum amount per month. On that basis if you make the occasional purchase and you don't pay off the balance in full each month you could be paying this type of credit for ever. Store cards, Visa and Access use revolving credit. This type is undoubtedly the most dangerous as you can end up paying interest on interest and a small debt can grow out of all proportion.

Credit reference agencies

At this stage it is worth mentioning these as they will almost automatically be referred to when credit is applied for.

How they work

Whenever you buy on credit someone has to find the money. Before doing so your credit-worthiness (how likely you are to be able to repay) has to be worked out. Many companies now use a system called credit scoring. You get points for certain information about yourself which increases the likelihood of you repaying. This is gathered from the questions you answer on the credit application form, and whether you attain a pass mark depends on your final score. There is therefore no single reason for being rejected.

Usually the retailer will get in touch with a credit reference agency. What these organizations do is to gather all relevant financial information about you. So, for example, it will have records of any court action taken against you for non-payment and may have notice of the fact that you have paid some clients slowly. The agency will not normally say whether you should or shouldn't be lent money. It will just give the retailer the facts it has about you.

Under the Consumer Credit Act you have the right to know what the agency is saying about you. If you believe what they are saying is factually incorrect you can try and put things right, especially if you are likely to suffer by not doing so. If this is your situation do not hesitate to ask for further information. As long as the credit you were trying to get is under £1500 you have the legal right to be given the name and address of any agency the retailer has consulted. The procedure is as follows:

1 Get the retailer to give you the name and address of the
   agency he consulted within 28 days of the time you were
   in touch about the deal. This should be in writing.
2 The retailer has seven working days in which to reply.
   He does NOT have to tell you what the agency said
   or what impact that had on his decision not to give
   credit.
3 Once you have the name and address you can ask the
   agency for a copy of the file they have about you. You
   need to ask for it in writing and enclose a £1 fee. Give as
   much information as you can to help them trace your file
   easily.
4 The agency must reply within seven working days. They
   will either tell you they have no file about you or they
   will send you a copy together with a statement of your
   rights.
5 Check the report thoroughly. If things in it are incorrect
   write again asking them to alter their records.
6 The agency should reply within 28 days. If they do not
   and they refuse to alter the file satisfactorily you can
   write your own note of correction. This should be less
   than 200 words. Send it to the agency and ask them to
   include it on your file.
7 You have 28 days to do this and they then have the same
   time in which to reply to you. As long as your correction
   is honest they should add it to your report.
8 If the agency either correct the report themselves or add
   your amendment to it they must send details of the
   correction to anyone who has enquired about your credit
   rating in the last six months. Equally they must also use
   the correction in the future.
9 If the time limits expire and the agency have not
   corrected their report, or have refused to accept your
   note of correction, then you can write to:

The Director General of Fair Trading
Field House
Breams Buildings
LONDON EC4A 1PR

Tell him:
a your name and address
b the name and address of the agency
c details of the incorrect entry
d why it is incorrect
e why you will suffer if it is not changed
f the (rough) date you sent the note of correction to the
   agency
g any further information, including copies of any correspondence

A copy of your letter will usually be forwarded to the
agency asking for comment. Either the matter will be
resolved or you will be able to see the reasons given for the
ongoing refusal to change your file.

   As you come to assess your debts in the next chapter it is
important that you remember these different sorts of credit
and the interest likely to be charged, as it will influence the
way you behave.

ACTION PLAN

1 **Write to creditors clarifying details of what you
   owe.**
2 **Ensure you write to your mortgage company.**
3 **Understand the basics of budgeting.**
4 **Start to prepare your own family budget.**

five

Practical Steps Continued – Assessing the Priorities

Having produced your budget you are now in a position to start looking at your debt situation. The first thing to do is simple: double-check that they really are your debts. Did you sign the agreement? Were you over eighteen at the time? Is there anybody else responsible? Is it an old debt that has suddenly appeared ten years after you should have paid it? In all the above you may be responsible for none or only part of the debt. In some cases too you may have taken out a one-off insurance policy to protect you in case you were ill or made redundant and then promptly forgotten about it. It really is worth checking thoroughly because you probably won't be advised of this. It is up to you to remember and up to you to claim. I recently had two cases like this in the course of one hour, and in one it meant the difference between keeping the company van or ceasing trading. Reading the small print of your agreement can make such a difference.

It is at this point that you need to have one last look at your income. Have you really put in everything you get on a regular basis? Have you had your meeting with the DSS and have they confirmed that you are getting everything to which you are entitled? Have you heard from the Inland Revenue about your request for a tax rebate? Are you sure your company paid you at least the minimum redundancy payments to which you are entitled under law?

Once you are sure you have received satisfactory answers to the above questions you need to make changes to your income and expenditure statement where appropriate. Replies from your creditors could lead to changes here too, but once all this has been done you are in a position to proceed.

It is important to realize that creditors will behave very differently. The more responsible, especially those with some form of security, will probably be sympathetic and try hard to help you. Others who have less recourse to get their money back may be less sympathetic, feeling they have to move quickly if there is to be any likelihood of them getting their money back. If you are unfortunate enough to have borrowed money from loan sharks you are especially likely to be put under pressure. Generally, you will find that those who bark the loudest have the least bite – do not be intimidated. However, you may be reading this book because you have been jolted into it by some particular thing that has happened. If it is something as serious as a fuel disconnection then you have to move straight away. Once the problem has been overcome and all your debts are back on an even footing it is time to prioritize your debts.

Listing your debts in order of priority

At the end of the day it is very much your individual decision as to what your priorities are. However, it is important to realize that not paying some debts can have much worse consequences than not paying others. Some of the worst things that can happen are:

> Loss of home – *eviction*
> Loss of services – *disconnection*
> Loss of possessions – *called distraint*
> and even Loss of liberty – *imprisonment*

Most of the above would only take place after exhaustive communication and lengthy court proceedings, but it is obviously important to deal with these matters as soon as possible. So you need to look at your list of debts and potential problem areas and then place them in order of importance to you. The list below should be a valuable help to you in this:

The worst that can happen:
Mortgage arrears.............................repossession/eviction
Second mortgages...........................repossession/eviction
Rent arrears ....eviction/distraint
Council Tax ....imprisonment/distraint
Water rates......................................disconnection
Gas or electricity ....disconnection
Unpaid fines....................................imprisonment
Maintenance arrears ....imprisonment
VAT arrears ....distraint
Hire purchase arrears.....................repossession without
(less than one-third paid)   court proceedings

There may be other things that are priorities to you that don't carry the same penalties. For example, a young mum with three small children would be keen to hang on to her washing machine, whilst others would find it essential to keep their phone to enable them to continue their work. However, keeping a roof over your head, staying warm and having water and light would be important to everyone.

As soon as you have drawn up your priorities you need to reschedule your list of debts into priority (i.e. leading to loss of home, facilities, goods or liberty) and non-priority. It could well look something like this:

Priority Debts		Non-priority Debts	
1 Mortgage	£3000	4 Bank overdraft	£800
2 Water	£500	5 Credit cards	£1000
3 Council Tax	£600	6 Store cards	£400

Congratulations! You have now identified your priority creditors. These are the ones you must be most concerned about and therefore you need to take any communication from them especially seriously. These are the ones that you are now going to concentrate on and work hardest to repay.

Before you look at the various priorities outlined it is important to remind yourself of the importance of communication – especially with these priority creditors who can do you so much damage. Hopefully, having completed your financial statement you will be in a position where you have at least some surplus to start paying off your priority debts. However, if you have just been made redundant, for example, and you haven't yet started receiving your benefit entitlement you may well find that you have no surplus. Don't panic, this should only be a temporary problem. You should soon get all the benefits sorted out and this should improve the situation considerably. For those who have no surplus and have worked through their budget and are convinced there is no extravagance or dishonesty there, you will have to allow things to take their course. Even given the low payment of many benefits this should only be a few of you. But your creditors, and possibly the court, will see your budget and probably come to the same conclusion as you – that you can't afford to pay anything off your debts at this time. If you are in this situation stay calm. You have probably already suffered some misfortune and most creditors and all courts should take this fully into consideration.

Without wanting to shatter your hopes at this stage it must be pointed out that, whatever your circumstances, you have probably already broken an agreement with your creditors. This means that in any negotiations they do not have to agree to any of your proposals. However, this doesn't mean that you shouldn't make any. Many creditors will accept them if they realize your situation has changed and that you are being honest with them. I was recently at a major building society where for every hundred cases of arrears only fifteen had written and explained their change of circumstances, offered a lower repayment figure and kept to it month after month. The staff there were far too busy constantly chasing the other 85%, who were either not replying or not keeping to agreements, and the staff were, therefore, quite content to leave the other 15% alone. After all, they had been honest and it was felt that as and when their lot improved they would do their utmost to repay their debts.

So, if your creditors do agree to take a new lower payment it is important that you do all in your power to keep to it. That is why it pays to be realistic. Any creditor would rather hear from you that you can pay £20 a month and see you stick to it, than get £30 one month, nothing the next and £10 the month after. Firstly, you are keeping your word. Secondly, you are making much less work for your creditor and thirdly it implies that you have your finances in some sort of order. If the situation changes again, i.e. you first get into difficulties because you were put on short time working and then later you lose your job, it is important to keep creditors informed each step of the way. If you need help go to your Citizen's Advice Bureau or Money Advice Centre. You will find their number in the phone book.

In the next chapter we'll look at the most common priority debts.

ACTION PLAN

1 **Identify which debts are more important to pay and why.**
2 **List your own debts into priority/non-priority columns.**

six

Priority Debts – Housing

Mortgages and second mortgages

Over the last fifteen years people in Britain have been encouraged to be part of a 'home-owning democracy'. As a result more and more switched from rented accommodation and there was thus a surge in first-time buyers. Many council house tenants were given significant incentives and discounts to buy their own home. Although for many this was an opportunity to be taken and not regretted, for too many it has brought problems and heartache. Some undoubtedly took on a commitment which proved to be too burdensome. The situation was made worse by the fact that as the difficulties grew and more and more families had to be rehoused, so there were far fewer council houses to use – they had mostly been sold to their existing tenants!

Undoubtedly, the high interest rates of the early 1990s led many to fall behind with their repayments. Other causes were a reduction in income, extra costs or problems at home. About 750,000 mortgages were more than two months or more behind in the 1991/92 period. This is one in twelve. It is vital to seek help if you are ever in danger of falling into this category. Homelessness creates all sort of hardship and misery. Much can be done to prevent it if you act in time.

Talk – having a roof over your and your family's head is almost certainly your major priority. Therefore, it is important to do all you can to build up a rapport with your lender. Don't be put off from contacting your lender just because you haven't been able to work out any proposals. There are a variety of things lenders can do to help. Even if you have been threatened with repossession it is important to remember that this will only be done as a very last step and when everything else has failed. You may even be able to get a court repossession order suspended if you make some proposals at that time, although it is much easier to sort things out well in advance of this.

Keep paying. Even when your situation appears hopeless you should still try to pay as much as you can towards your mortgage. This should not only mean that your arrears do not rise too sharply but will also give a clear indication to your mortgage company of just how seriously you take paying your mortgage. Surprisingly many people think that if they can't manage the full amount there is no point in paying anything as their lender will only accept it all. This certainly is not the case.

Relationship breakdown. If your relationship has broken down immediately inform your lender of your difficulties. Make sure your ex-partner is not trying to use your home as security for borrowing more or even trying to sell it. Try to make some payment. If you are not working, or doing only limited hours, you should apply to the Department of Social Security for Income Support. They may well be able to help you by paying the interest payments due on the mortgage.

Warning. Whatever problems you may be facing it is vital that you keep communicating and do nothing silly. You may, for example, be tempted to pay off your existing mortgage and clear your other debts by taking on a larger mortgage with another lender. If you are thinking of doing this seek independent advice first. You may in effect be making some unsecured loans (which have limited legal redress) into secured loans and, therefore, increasing the possibility of losing your home. Some re-mortgage packages are so unsuited to borrowers on low incomes they should be avoided at all costs. On the other hand, if by re-mortgaging you are taking in a finance company debt which is already secured on your property you may save sufficient interest to be able to balance your monthly budget. Suffice it to say that most building societies are now ready, willing and able to look at your individual circumstances and offer you what they consider to be the best possible option. Let's look at some of these now, beginning with the very basis of how a mortgage works.

Definition
A mortgage is a loan which is secured on your house and is repayable within an agreed number of years (usually twenty-five).

Legal charge. To protect itself the lender will apply a legal charge on the property. This means that if you fall behind on your agreed payments the lender can apply to the court to sell your home. All charges (mortgages, secured loans, etc.) have to be removed before the property can be sold, and thus all outstanding monies owed, including interest and arrears, have to be repaid when the property is sold. Each charge is registered in the order in which the money is borrowed, and lenders are repaid in that order when the home is sold. That is why when house prices were falling in the early 1990s it was often the second mortgage companies who were pressing for repossession as they could see that they might end up with very little after the first mortgage was paid off. In theory if the charges add up to more than the price the house sells for, the last lender will be able to pursue you as he tries to recover the balance owed. In practice many of you will have nothing to give and therefore most of these types of loan will eventually be written off. But it will not be surprising if, when unemployment drops as economic recovery takes place, some lenders will be chasing creditors years after they have lost their homes.

How does a mortgage work?

The mortgage agreement doesn't just safeguard the lender's right to repossess your home. It also gives details of the amount borrowed and sets out the terms on which the loan is meant to be repaid. The monthly payment will be made up of two parts:

1 *Interest* – the price, in effect, you are paying for borrowing the money.
2 *Capital Repayment* or *Endowment Premium* – the means by which the money borrowed will be repaid.

Capital repayment mortgage

This is the simplest type of mortgage and in many cases the best. The monthly instalment (interest and repayment) is calculated to ensure that the loan is repaid within the given period. As each year passes the amount owing is reduced and thus the interest payment is less. This means every year you are reducing the capital owed. Remember, however, that each time you move you are restarting this process and it is only in the later years of this kind of mortgage that you will be repaying any significant capital.

Endowment mortgage

Unlike the capital repayment mortgage, the endowment mortgage does not provide for the full amount borrowed to be repaid at the end of the term. The monthly payment paid direct to the lender is interest only. Thus the amount owing to the lender will not change if full payments are maintained. To ensure that the borrower can repay the loan at the end of the term the lender will want suitable endowment policies taken out with a life assurance company which will pay back the full capital sum borrowed in a lump sum at the end of the mortgage.

Unlike the capital repayment mortgage, there is no need for you to arrange a mortgage protection policy as the loan is fully repaid if you die during the mortgage term, although sickness and redundancy cover should still be considered. This applies to all four major types of endowment policy:

1 *Low cost, low start* – payments are kept lower than average for the first five years, although they will increase in each of those years. They will then level off at an amount higher than the ordinary low-cost endowment. They are not guaranteed to repay the loan by the end of the term.
2 *Low cost* – these are not guaranteed to pay the loan.
3 *Unit-linked* – payments are made each month to purchase unit funds managed by the insurance company. The loan is repaid when it has sufficiently gained in value. This is not necessarily by the end of the mortgage.
3 *Full with profits* – payments are set at a level which should guarantee the loan is repaid by the end of the term and could also provide an extra lump sum.

Endowment mortgages by their very nature are harder to renegotiate as they are tied in to insurance contracts and this is just one reason to think hard before taking on such a mortgage. The percentage of policies that actually receive their terminal bonus is very low.

Tax relief on mortgage interest payments (MIRAS)

Since August 1988 tax relief has only been given on the interest due on the first £30,000 of home purchase loans. However, if you purchased a property jointly with someone else to whom you were not married before that time you can still both claim the maximum tax relief. Many young couples, who were given six months' advance warning of this change, rushed to purchase houses in this period thus providing an artificial stimulus to the housing market and also making a rod for their own (and others') backs as prices started to fall shortly afterwards. Relationship breakdowns have added to these problems. Tax relief is also given on home improvements loans taken out prior to April 1988. If you fall into either category you almost certainly should not even consider remortgaging your property as you will lose a lot of your tax relief. Nearly all mortgages will allow the lender to take the tax relief into account when calculating the mortgage payments. This is known as Mortgage Interest Relief At Source (MIRAS).

The effects of high interest rates

The cost of borrowing in the summer of 1988 was 9.75%. Not long afterwards it had jumped to 15.4%. The effect of this was devastating. For example, an unmarried couple who had got tax relief on the full amount of their £60,000 mortgage would have seen their monthly payment jump from £365 to £575 a month – a 60% increase. Some lenders alter interest rates only yearly. This can be good news if rates are going up, but the reverse is equally true.

The effects of losing MIRAS

One of the anomalies of a government that supports 'family values' is that if you marry a joint occupier you will have your maximum MIRAS entitlement halved! Depending on interest rates this could cost you between £15 and £30 each month for every £10,000 you have borrowed.

Negotiating with your lender

By talking honestly to your lender and giving all relevant facts you may well find you will be presented with an option that will help you. It is well worth giving your lender an up-to-date valuation of your property. Most local estate agents will do this free of charge. This can help in a variety of ways. For example, if you have a lot of equity in your house you may persuade the lender to add any arrears to the value of the mortgage. This is called capitalization of arrears. Here is an example:

> Tom had got into arrears when he lost his overtime, but this had just been restored. He had his house valued and found it was worth £55,000. His mortgage was £30,000 so he had equity of £25,000. The lender agreed to add on the £3,000 arrears to his mortgage, making it £33,000. He had to make slightly higher monthly payments, but he was able to afford them as his overtime had been restored.

On the other hand, if your property has fallen in value and is now worth less than the mortgage you are not giving your lender much incentive to repossess it! As long as you are trying to make some sort of regular payment they are likely to wait in the hope that your situation improves.

It is important as well to try and negotiate with someone senior – someone who has both the authority and flexibility to make decisions. In practice this will usually be your local branch office manager or someone in authority at head office. Remember to make a note of their name and keep communicating with the same person.

Whatever solution the lender finally comes up with depends on your individual circumstances. These will include your income and outgoings, the value of your property, the amount outstanding on the mortgage, the arrears (if any), the type of mortgage, the length of any other outstanding loans secured on the property, whether your problems appear long- or short-term and the attitude of your lender.

It is essential, therefore, that any proposals you put forward are realistic and are likely to bring about a solution without increasing the risk to your lender.

Cutting your costs – endowment mortgage
As mentioned earlier, the payments due to this type of mortgage fall into two parts:

1 **Endowment premiums**. It may be possible to persuade your insurance company to change the type of policy you have. For example, you could switch from a 'full with profits' policy to a 'low start' endowment, or if your policy was short-term you could extend it to a longer period. Equally, if you have been paying the premiums for many years and are confident that your problems are temporary, you might be allowed to stop paying for a few months and catch up when your problems are behind you. (This is called a contribution holiday.)

If, however, none of these options helps much as you are just unable to pay your monthly endowment premiums, you should consider changing to a repayment mortgage. As stated earlier, if the policy has been running for more than a couple of years it could well have some surrender value. If you do not keep up your payments the insurance company will automatically lapse the policy, and your lender could then convert your mortgage to a repayment one

SMART MOVE 3

The Need for Good Budgeting

Harry and Sally had done everything wrong. They
had moved into their home with a £40,000 mortgage
two years ago. Harry had tried to do the accounts but
then found that they did not appear to be able to live
on their income so he gave up. Sadly, he didn't
inform Sally of this, so she continued to spend in
blissful ignorance. Soon they had run up arrears of
£1,200 on their mortgage plus other debts amounting
to £4,000. Sally earned £600 a month and Harry
£120 a week. In desperation Harry turned to the
lender for assistance only to be told that it was far too
late – he had ignored letters, and repossession
proceedings would commence unless the full arrears
were cleared in the next fourteen days.

Sheepishly Harry had to tell Sally, and he was glad
he did. She stormed into action, firstly deciding that
from then on she would be in charge of all the bills.
She contacted the building society, promising that as
they could manage on her income all of Harry's
would be paid into the mortgage account. This was
enough to cover the ordinary instalment, interest due
on the arrears and repay most of the arrears at the
rate of £25 a month. Having done that she went to the
local Citizens' Advice Bureau and they were able to
help her with the remaining debts. Most were credit
card companies and they were persuaded to stop
charging interest. Debt payments were thus reduced
substantially, and from a picture of dark despair both
Harry and Sally could see light at the end of the
tunnel.

which would mean, in theory, having to start paying off the capital as well as the interest. Before you finally decide to switch make sure you have exhausted all options with your insurance company, as well as seeing if your lender will delay charging for the capital element to give you a breathing space.

SMART MOVES 4

Switch from Endowment to Repayment

Peter lived in a two-bedroomed flat which he had bought two years ago with an endowment mortgage of £40,000. He put down a deposit of £1,200 – virtually all the money he had. Sadly Peter's boss had to stop all overtime because of the recession and Peter's income fell by £100 a month. At the same time he received a demand for a special maintenance charge of £500 as the entire building's drainage had to be replaced. Peter did not have enough money to pay the current month's mortgage and certainly couldn't afford the maintenance charge. He earned £10,500 a year.

Peter managed to convince his lender that he should switch from an endowment to a repayment mortgage. He thus allowed his endowment policy to lapse. In addition the lender agreed to accept interest-only payments for six months. This saved Peter about £75 a month. The lender also agreed to pay the maintenance charge of £500 and this was added to the amount of mortgage outstanding.

At the end of the six months period Peter would revert to a normal repayment mortgage which would be repaid either by the return of overtime payments or by taking in a lodger.

---

2 Interest. It is possible your lender can be pressured to accept reduced payments of interest for a limited period in the following circumstances:

a To allow the maintenance of the endowment policy if your problems are likely to be short-term or if the policy is very near to its maturity date.
b If you or your partner are seriously ill.
c If you are trying to sell your home.

Arrears will build up in these cases, but they can either be added to the mortgage (capitalized) or repaid over an agreed period.

Cutting your costs – repayment mortgage
1 Capital repayment. As the size of these repayments depends on how long you have to repay the money borrowed, you can save money in the short-term in two ways:

a By extending the repayment term.
b By stopping the capital repayments (interest only).

If you can persuade your lender to do either of these your payments can be reduced significantly. Should your situation improve or interest rates fall you can ask your lender to revert to the original position. If the lender does agree to stop all capital repayments for a limited time make sure that the capital is suspended or arrears will build up.

2 Interest. Again your lender may be prepared to accept lower interest payments if your position is likely to improve soon and if you are trying to sell your home. When you make proposals which will lead to arrears it is important that you always suggest that they are added to the mortgage at the end of any concessionary period.

SMART MOVE 5

Interest Only and Short-term Adjustment

Jack and Jill bought their home a year ago with a £40,000 repayment mortgage. Jill stopped working two months ago to have a baby, but she expects to be back at work in ten months' time. Jill's income of £300 a month was relied on so they were struggling to pay their mortgage. Jack earned £7,500 a year.

First, Jack and Jill asked the building society to switch their mortgage to interest-only payments, saving them £30 a month. But the building society also agreed to accept reduced payments of £300 a month for a period of one year. Thus their mortgage payments were effectively reduced by £130 a month for the period that Jill would not be working. At the end of that time the mortgage repayments will be recalculated to allow for the money owed to be repaid over the balance of the mortgage period. The new payments would only add about £12 a month to their mortgage.

Borrow extra to clear debts

If you are struggling to pay your main mortgage because of other more expensive, short-term loans secured on your home, you might be able to get your mortgage lender to give you extra time to repay them. By charging a lower interest and spreading the payments over a longer period your expenditure should reduce to a more manageable level.

Think twice, however, if you have loans that are currently unsecured. You may well pay less, but you are securing your home against a higher loan and if you start missing payments you could lose your home. So never try and borrow more than you need.

REMEMBER – NEVER STOP PAYING – ALWAYS PAY A REGULAR AMOUNT EACH MONTH

Opening negotiations yourself

If your lender has not come up with any proposals of his own or if your situation is relatively simple, you might have to work out your own proposals and persuade the lender that they are reasonable. To help you do so you need to be able to answer the following questions:

1 Are my difficulties short- or long-term?
2 Is it realistic to stay in my home or should I try and sell it?
3 How much can I afford to pay the lender each month?
4 How confident am I of maintaining these payments?
5 How will the proposal affect my arrears position?

When you have satisfactorily answered these questions yourself you need to write to your local branch manager explaining your difficulties and putting forward a revised proposal. Your letter should include the following:

1 Your financial statement as well as a list of all debts.
2 An explanation of the steps you have already taken to improve your financial position.
3 Proposals of how you wish to change your mortgage payments and the impact this will have.
4 Where appropriate, show how a further advance would help you pay off expensive short-term loans and what reduction in your expenditure would result.
5 An explanation of what the future holds and why a change at this stage would be helpful to you.
6 Where a sale is necessary, the amount you can afford to pay each month and the amount you are hoping to get for your house.

Negotiating a settlement – a summary

1 Talk to your lender and discuss any difficulties.
2 Ensure you are maximizing income and minimizing expenditure.
3 Follow up phone calls with letters and keep copies.
4 Don't be afraid of the lender rejecting your proposals.
5 Always pay a regular sum towards the mortgage each month.
6 Never offer to pay what you cannot really afford.

How to annoy your lenders!

1 Do not reply to letters.
2 Do not contact them until the very last moment, especially after court proceedings have commenced.
3 Do not tell them about your difficulties, even if they could help you.
4 Do not be truthful about other debts.
5 Make unrealistic offers which you have no hope of keeping to.

The arrears procedure

Stage one – first missed payment
You will receive a letter informing you of the missed payment and asking you to sort out the matter. You will be encouraged to talk to the lender about any difficulties you may be facing. This letter will be friendly.

Stage two – more missed payments
If you continue to miss payments and fail to reach agreement with your lender you will get increasingly 'firmer' letters until eventually you will be threatened with legal action. In this you will be advised that unless you

bring your account completely up to date in seven days or
reach agreement, solicitors will be instructed to commence
possession proceedings.

Stage three – referred to lender's solicitors

If you do not respond to your lender's letter you will
receive a letter from their solicitor advising you that you
have seven days to pay in full or else repossession
proceedings will be commenced without further notice.

Stage four – possession summons issued

Within a few weeks of this letter you will receive a
Possession Summons by the County Court. This will give
you the place, date and time of the hearing. It is important
you attend, or you will almost certainly lose your home.
Details of the workings of the court will be found later in
the book.

The lender's attitude to your arrears

This will be influenced by a variety of factors including:

1 The time and effort they have had to spend on your
   arrears problem.
2 Your ability, or otherwise, to stop or slow down any
   increase in arrears.
3 What, if any, equity is in the property.
4 Whether you can reach an agreement with the lender
   and stick to it.
5 How easy it will be to repossess (and how costly) if you
   fail to make arrangements.

A lender will usually be very reluctant to repossess your
home, but may sometimes seek a court order which will
be suspended. This is to exert maximum pressure on you

to maintain the agreed payments. You only need to miss one more payment and the lender can apply for a warrant of possession.

How to clear your arrears
There are basically three ways this can be done:

1 **Lump sum.** If you can raise a lump sum – by cashing in an endowment policy for example – it may be possible to clear all or part of the arrears. Whatever you do *don't borrow more to pay off the arrears* – unless the new loan is at a much lower rate of interest.

2 **Instalments.** If your financial situation has improved since the arrears built up – you could be back in full-time work for example – your lender may agree to you paying back the arrears over an agreed period by paying an amount on top of the ordinary instalment. Try and take as long as you need to pay off the arrears without putting yourself under further severe pressure.

3 **Adding arrears to the mortgage.** After proving that you are again able to meet the normal mortgage payments by maintaining payments for, say, a six-month period, your lender could agree to add your arrears to the mortgage so that you have the rest of the term to pay them off. The advantage of this is that only interest is payable on the sum of the arrears until the end of the term. The interest on £2,000 of arrears, for example, could be less than £15 a month.

The most common way of referring to this sort of agreement is 'capitalizing' the arrears. By adding the arrears to the mortgage you are, in effect, being offered a completely new start.

Obviously, it is possible to use any combination of the above three methods to come to a satisfactory conclusion.

SMART MOVE 6

Slow Arrears Repayments

Kevin and Neil bought their home with a £55,000 endowment mortgage in 1988. At the time both were working full-time, but Neil was made redundant and did not find work for six months. During that time he did not pay his share of the mortgage as he had failed to claim Income Support. By the time he found work arrears were approximately £2,000 as Kevin had been paying less on the mortgage in order to keep up payments on the endowment. Kevin was earning £12,000 a year and Neil £9,500.

Although Kevin and Neil had considered re-mortgaging with another lender they would have lost the benefit of the extra MIRAS (Double tax relief was only allowed for mortgages taken out before August 1988). They would also have had to meet the cost of re-arranging the mortgage. However, as they are now able to meet their endowment and interest payments in full it has been agreed that they can pay off the arrears at a rate of £50 a month.

Arrears and MIRAS

If your mortgage is six months or £1000 in arrears (whichever is the lower), your lender is legally required to inform the Inland Revenue unless you have made arrangements to which the lender has agreed to clear the arrears. In reality the lender may delay in the hope that a solution can be found – and also because they will continue to get at least the tax relief of the mortgage whilst it is in MIRAS.

However, if the mortgage is taken out of MIRAS your lender will automatically increase your payments to reflect the fact that you should pay the full interest due. If this

---

SMART MOVE 7

Capitalization

Brian and Jennifer bought their home five years ago with the help of a £30,000 endowment mortgage. Jennifer stopped work a year ago to have a baby and does not expect to return to work for at least another two years. They had kept up their mortgage payments but had debts of £5,000, including a £4,000 loan which was secured on the property and was three months in arrears. They had received a letter threatening legal action over this particular loan.

Brian was earning £14,000 a year. The house was worth £42,000. The interest rate on their loan was twice that of their mortgage.

Brian and Jennifer persuaded their lender to up their mortgage by £5,000. They were thus able to pay off all their existing debts, including the expensive loan. Not only that, but the significant reduction in their interest charges meant that they were able to live on Brian's salary and could thus keep up all their payments, including the mortgage.

---

happens, contact the Inland Revenue immediately so that you can claim tax relief through an adjustment of your tax coding on what you do pay.

Arrears and Income Support

During the first sixteen weeks, half of your mortgage interest payments should be paid directly to you in the form of Income Support. Ensure that you use it to keep making payments on your mortgage. After sixteen weeks the full amount of your mortgage interest should be paid from

Income Support directly to your lender. After sixteen weeks have elapsed it is worth checking that this is indeed happening.

Arrears – a summary
1 Never stop making payments on a mortgage.
2 Make regular monthly payments, however small.
3 Don't ignore any communication from your lender.
4 Don't be put off by an initial negative response from your lender.
5 Always inform your lender of any difficulties.
6 Always put forward reasonable proposals.
7 NEVER take a short-term, high interest loan to clear arrears.

REMEMBER – TALK TO YOUR LENDER.

WARNING! Do not just abandon your property or hand the keys back to the lender. The property remains your responsibility until it is sold. While it remains unsold the mortgage payments will continue to accumulate. On top of that the lender will have estate agent and legal costs which he will claim from you. Remember too that an empty, unfurnished house is likely to realize far less than one that is lived in.

Having to sell your home
Very occasionally all these strategies may fail. If your arrears are mounting and negotiation has failed you may have to sell your property. If you do it is important to do the following:

1 Check how much is outstanding on all charges registered on the property.
2 Ask your solicitor and estate agent for the likely sale cost.

3 Put a realistic value on your house.
4 If the sale proceeds are insufficient to repay all the
  money owed, talk to all lenders and creditors who are
  affected, and try to ensure you reach agreement. They
  may even write off some of the debt.

Second mortgages

Many of you will have second mortgages secured on
your home. Remember, these companies can ask for a
possession order just as easily. Given that the first lender
will be paid first they will probably be keener to go for
repossession. It is, therefore, important that you contact
them as soon as problems arise and try and reach
agreement. With most second mortgages you will be
dealing with a 'centralized' lender and, therefore, will need
to send concise letters rather than rely on building up a
personal relationship with someone local.

It could be worth trying to overcome the problem of a
second mortgage by increasing the size of the first. It is
certainly worth asking.

Rent arrears

When you are under financial pressure it is very easy to
miss a week's rent. But these arrears can build up very
quickly. Eventually your landlord (whether private or
council) will decide that they have to start eviction
proceedings. These will be looked at later on, but it is
important to say that if you are evicted it will be very
difficult to find another place to live. Councils are not
obliged to rehouse you if you have been evicted for rent
arrears, and private landlords would expect a reference
from your previous landlord. Therefore, eviction is to be
avoided at all costs.

SMART MOVE 8

Securing Second Loans

Olive and Clive purchased their home a year ago with the assistance of a £25,000 endowment mortgage and soon after took out a further loan with a finance company to install double glazing. Sadly, Clive was badly injured in a car accident shortly afterwards and was told he would not be able to work for eighteen months. He received Income Support for his loans but had to find cash to pay back the finance company over the five-year period. By now Olive and Clive had used all their savings in keeping up their payments.

At first it appeared that they had been badly advised, so the building society allowed them to cancel their endowment policy. However, they were still unable to meet the capital repayment of £65 a month from their sick pay and Income Support. The finance company would not alter the terms of the loan so the building society advanced a further £5,000 to repay the double glazing loan early. The arrears were thus kept static and will be capitalized when Clive eventually goes back to work. In the meantime, the building society's generous action saved them around £150 a month.

Council tenants. A council tenant is someone who lives in public property. The local council will usually be sympathetic towards those with rent arrears so it is important to keep communicating. Try to maintain payments so that arrears don't mount up. It may be in certain cases that the house you are in has become too big, and you might request a move to a smaller place where the rent is lower. In other cases your low income will entitle you to Housing Benefit which will help considerably.

Private tenants. Private landlords are usually much more strict than councils when it comes to rent arrears. This is often because they depend on the income for their own living. Despite this, or perhaps because of it, keep talking and making offers that you can afford. If you feel your rent is too high you can apply to the Rent Officer to have a fair rent registered on your house. This means that the landlord cannot increase your rent without returning to the Rent Officer for a review.

Remember too that if you get Housing Benefit and/or Income Support you can have it paid direct to your landlord. This should make him more amenable to any offer you propose, as it would mean that at least the situation would not deteriorate further. If your landlord refuses to accept your reasonable offer, still start paying what you can afford. This should help if the landlord decides to take court action.

Private landlords also have another course of action open to them – distraint. This entitles the landlord to ask a private bailiff to visit your home and take possession of your belongings until you have paid the arrears. If you do not pay within the seven days the possessions are sold at auction, and after the costs of the auctioneers, bailiffs and landlord you will be lucky to get anything back. Fortunately, this is only used as a last resort, but once the bailiffs have removed your possessions only a substantial offer to pay off the arrears quickly will halt proceedings.

Bullying landlords

Nearly all of you will have heard horror stories of bullying landlords. It is important to remember that:

1 A landlord cannot evict you from your property without first going to court and obtaining a court order.
2 You cannot be harassed, frightened or bullied.
3 You cannot be telephoned late at night, subjected to repeated visits, threatened with violence or presented with 'official-looking' documents.
4 You cannot be prosecuted in the criminal courts.

All of the above are offences under Section 40 of the Administration of Justice Act 1970. If any of these ever happen to you, complain to both the Trading Standards Department and the police.

Housing rights for homeless people

Sadly, there will be a very few cases where either the situation has been allowed to continue for far too long or there has been a dramatic deterioration in circumstances. If this applies to you seek help urgently from your local council.

Making a homeless application

You are entitled to make an application to the local authority of your choice, but if you do not have a strong connection with the area they can refer your case to another district where you do. If you are homeless, or likely to be so within the next twenty-eight days, the local authority have to accept your application.

Priority needs
Only those listed below have a right to be provided with accommodation by law. They are:

1 Pregnant women.
2 Households with dependent children.
3 Anyone who is vulnerable as a result of old age, mental handicap or physical disability.
4 Anyone who has lost their home as a result of an emergency such as fire or flood.
5 Victims of domestic violence.

Intentionally homeless
Remember, if you deliberately do something – like handing your keys back to your lender – or fail to do something which leads to you becoming homeless, the council can rule that you did it on purpose. This means that it has a duty to provide only very limited assistance, even if you are in priority need.

Assistance with re-housing
Housing departments must notify you of their decision in writing. If their decision is unfavourable reasons must be given and you have the right to appeal.

Given the severe shortage of council homes many homeless applicants have to remain in temporary accommodation, such as bed and breakfast, before being offered permanent housing. This can last for years. It is also worth applying to local housing associations, although it is likely that their waiting lists will be at least as long.

Summary of homeless applications
1 Not in priority need – council will give advice only.
2 No local connection, but in priority need and not intentionally homeless – temporary accommodation for

a short time, pending referral to another local authority with which you have a connection.

3 No local connection, in priority need but intentionally homeless – temporary accommodation for a short time only with no referral.

4 Local connection, in priority need, but intentionally homeless – temporary accommodation for a short time only.

5 Local connection, in priority need and not intentionally homeless – temporary accommodation provided pending permanent rehousing, unless you solve your problem in the meantime.

It cannot be stressed enough, however, that if your debt problems are faced as soon as they threaten to appear, and honest communication takes place with your creditors, then hardly anyone should find themselves homeless.

ACTION PLAN

1 **Communicate with your mortgage company or landlord, having understood the various options available to you.**
2 **Try to negotiate an agreement with them that is acceptable to both of you.**

seven

Other Priorities

In addition to your housing debts you may well have several others. Again it is important to look at them in your order of priority. Those that will be of importance to you will probably include:

1 **Gas and/or electricity bills.** These are of great concern to many of us, particularly the elderly and young mothers. Especially during cold weather very large bills can quickly mount up. Ironically it is the old, the poor, the unemployed, who are at home all day and need to keep warm, who have the biggest bills.

The companies concerned are very powerful. They can disconnect in a matter of weeks after the arrears first occur. They have an automatic right of entry, so it is important, as with all creditors, to talk to them immediately a problem arises. The companies will do everything they can to help you find a solution because they regard disconnections as a very last resort. Send them your financial statement and try and negotiate with them. Often bad publicity rebounds on them, especially if they disconnect an elderly person or a mother with young children. So if you fall into either category make sure they are aware of your circumstances.

There is a code of practice designed to protect extreme hardship cases. Let either the Social Services or Social Security know about your situation, and ask them for help. Let the fuel company know you are doing this as well.

They should then postpone disconnection for at least fourteen days to give them more time to help you.

There are several ways in which you can avoid the shock of a large bill. You can purchase stamps on a regular basis or make regular payments in advance, but sometimes even this is not enough. In this case it could well be worth considering the use of prepayment slot meters. These can even be set to enable you to pay part of your debt every time you use them. Their big advantage is that you will no longer have to face unexpectedly expensive bills, and you will also be able to monitor on a daily basis the amount of fuel you are using. They can, therefore, be a great aid to help you discipline your fuel spending. There are some disadvantages, however, and these include:

1 You may have to pay for the installation.
2 You may not be allowed a meter if you live in an area which has a high crime rate.
3 If you are burgled you may have to pay again.
4 You may be charged a higher rate for the arrears component of your payment.
5 You may have to go without heat and light in winter if you have no money available at the time.

Despite these negatives, however, they are proving helpful to a considerable number of people.

It is always worth having your meter checked, especially if bill after bill seems higher than you expected. If the meter is found to be faulty you will be entitled to a refund. However, without wanting to dash your hopes, I have to tell you that this is very rare and it is much more likely that fuel is being used uneconomically. Below are some guidelines for reducing your fuel bills:

1 Always switch off a light when you leave a room.

2 Use low-wattage bulbs where appropriate.
3 Use your immersion heater as little as possible (these are likely to be the major cause of high electricity bills) – lag your tank and lower the thermostat after checking that it is working properly.
4 Avoid electric fires where possible.
5 Check whether your local electricity board is running any schemes for obtaining cheaper electricity that would be suitable for your needs.
6 Check with British Gas that your installations are as efficient as they can be.

Gas and electricity officials do have the right to enter your home once they have obtained a warrant, but are only likely to cut you off when arrears have built up and you have refused to answer their many demands. As already indicated, if you have been cut off check with the council Social Services Department or the Benefits Agency to see if they can help. If not, you will have to make some sort of arrangement to pay off your arrears before a supply will be reconnected. In addition you may have to pay a deposit as well as a reconnection charge. These could be reduced however if you intend to use a prepayment meter which has been pre-set to recover some of your debt. You can also be sued for the debt.

2 **Water.** Water charges are fixed for the twelve months commencing on 1 April each year and are usually paid in two half-yearly instalments in April and October. If you do not reach agreement with the water company it can apply to the court for permission to disconnect your water supply. The company can also take legal action to recover the debt as well as demand a reconnection fee and deposit. Despite the obvious health dangers there has been a recent increase in the number of disconnections, which has caused considerable adverse press comment. In about

75% of cases, however, this is 'short, sharp shock treatment' and the water is reconnected almost immediately when communication finally gets under way.

You should find all water companies sympathetic to your problems and they should give you a reasonable period of grace. Again it is important to keep in touch, and do remember to tell them if any of your family have special needs, e.g. children, elderly or disabled. All relevant facts will help your case.

3 **Council Tax/Poll Tax arrears.** The Community Charge (Poll Tax) was introduced in April 1990 to replace the domestic rates system. It proved to be so unpopular, uncollectable and thus unsuccessful that it was replaced in 1993 by the Council Tax. Ignoring many exemptions, and put very simply, every working adult over the age of eighteen who lived in the same community paid the same amount of tax irrespective of their earnings and the type of property or area they lived in. Although it could be argued that everyone had use of the same facilities in their community, it put an immense strain on the lower paid and was thus widely regarded as unfair. It was replaced with the Council Tax which, although it does not have people shouting from the rooftops, is certainly regarded as more equitable. With this tax all houses are put into bands according to their value and then a rate is struck for each band. The charge is also for each property rather than per person. In both cases there are reductions and exemptions for different bands of people such as the unemployed, disabled or in the case of Council Tax a single person. Always check to see if you qualify. Remember, the Council Tax, like the Poll Tax, is paid by the tenant not the landlord!

Paying either of these taxes should be a priority because if you do not pay it could eventually lead to court action. It is probable that a Liability Order will be applied for. This enables the council to instruct bailiffs to remove goods from your home in order that they may be sold to clear your debt (known as distraint). The court could also issue an Attachment of Earnings Order which means that your employer would be required to make a deduction from your salary before you received it. Equally, they may ask the DSS effectively to do the same by deducting money from any Income Support you may receive.

It is worth knowing that husbands and wives and unmarried couples living together as man and wife are considered to be mutually liable for one another's bills. So if one partner falls behind with his or her payments or leaves, the other partner could be held liable to pay. In rare cases too the council may ask the court to imprison those from whom it has failed to recover the money by all methods available. The sentence will depend on how much you owe, and unlike unpaid fines is a punishment for nonpayment. So you will still owe the arrears when the sentence is over. In practice if you have been communicating with your council this should not occur.

4 Ground rent and maintenance. If you own a leasehold property – usually a flat or maisonette – you will be required to pay ground rent and maintenance charge to the freeholder or their managing agent. The consequences of not paying these are very serious as the freeholder can apply to the court for the forfeiture of the lease. This would mean that not only would you lose the right to occupy your home, but the property would be worthless to you unless the freeholder agreed to offer a new lease to a prospective purchaser.

If you are experiencing difficulties, and it is possible to be suddenly hit by large one-off maintenance charges, try and get agreement to pay by instalments. If this fails and you have a mortgage it is well worth asking your lender to meet the debt, which could be added to your mortgage. It is obviously not in their interests either for your property to become worthless.

5 **Telephone.** Telephone bills can be a major source of worry – and, particularly if you have teenage children, quite often a shock as well! If you are in debt you could consider getting rid of the phone altogether so that you can cut down on your expenses. You could well have reasons that make it essential to have a phone, however. Your job or your well-being may depend on it. If this is the case try and keep your calls as short as possible, and make them during the cheap rate period.

Phone bills should normally be paid within four weeks of being issued. If you do not reach agreement with British Telecom your telephone will be disconnected shortly after a final demand has been issued. You will then face legal action as well as a reconnection charge.

If you feel the bill really is exceptionally high, the exchange machinery can be checked and your phone monitored to see if the high usage is continuing. BT will usually insist that they are right. That is because they usually are. It is far more likely that someone may be using your phone without your knowledge. Where does your babysitter's boyfriend live!!? To counter this you can buy a phone lock from the Telecom showroom or arrange for your phone to receive incoming calls only.

Whatever your problem, try and come to an agreement with British Telecom to pay off your arrears by instalments. You should also arrange to pay future bills on a more regular basis – either by paying by standing order or by buying telephone stamps. In both cases this could be done on a monthly basis.

6 **Unpaid fines.** If you do not pay your fines this can lead to an order for your arrest. You will have to give an account of why the fine has not been paid, and if it isn't satisfactory you can be imprisoned straight away. You obviously should take your financial statement with you and ask the court to take it into account. If you are

sentenced to imprisonment the amount of the fine that you owe decreases daily. Payment of the remaining debt will ensure your release.

It is never pleasant having to go to court, but in these situations it is especially worrying. Get there in plenty of time. Take your financial statement, together with a list of all your other debts and any copies of letters you have showing negotiated agreements with other creditors. Hand these in to the magistrates' clerk so that the magistrates have time to read them and they can then appreciate your efforts. It would be a good idea to try and get someone from your local Law Centre or Citizens' Advice Bureau to accompany you.

7 **Maintenance.** As soon as you realize that you will be unable to keep up your maintenance payments, or if arrears start to accrue, apply to the court for a variation of the order. Take along your financial statement and schedule of debts to the clerk and make a new offer. The clerk will consider the offer and put it to all interested parties. If agreement is reached then there is no need for another hearing. If not, you will be summoned before the court where the magistrates will make their decision. They have the power to reduce payments and even write off arrears if they feel your situation has deteriorated badly since the last hearing.

8 **Hire purchase.** A hire purchase agreement hires goods to the customer for an agreed period, at the end of which you have an option to purchase them, usually at nominal value. As such, therefore, goods bought in this way do not always rank as a priority debt. However, if you need your car for your job or your washing machine to cater for the needs of a young family these debts can be of priority and you should argue that the item really is needed.

It is important to remember that when you enter a hire purchase agreement you do not own the items until you have made the final payment. As a result, if you sell the goods during the time you are making payments, without the permission of the seller, you will be committing an offence. If you default on your payments the hirer can repossess the goods, but will need a court order to do so if you have paid more than one-third of the purchase price. Things will work in your favour here if:

1 The resale value of any repossessed goods is generally poor. If this is the case, and it usually is, it is well worth trying to negotiate reduced payments with the HP company.
2 You are making regular payments (even at a reduced level). The court will usually be reluctant to grant repossession orders if you are seen to be making an effort to pay.

It is important that you let other priority creditors know why these items are vital possessions for you.

9 **Tax and VAT and National Insurance contributions.** These debts are a priority because both the Inland Revenue and Customs can seize goods from you to cover unpaid tax without needing a court order. Both can even instigate bankruptcy proceedings, as well as forcing court action. If you do not keep to the terms of the court order for income tax, but can afford to do so, you can be imprisoned for contempt of court. But with VAT arrears there also has to be fraud.

National Insurance contributions are priorities for the self-employed among you, as they are assessed and collected by the same people in the Inland Revenue who collect your unpaid income tax.

Trying to negotiate with government bodies – and especially the taxman – is never easy. You can only send them your financial statement and make an offer which could be acceptable.

10 **Personal debts to family, friends, etc.** Most of these will be unsecured and low priority. However, for compelling personal reasons there may well be exceptions. For example, it would be a priority to repay a family debt if it threatened to shatter the relationship. Such creditors may themselves be in debt to a priority creditor and without that money would be in major difficulty.

In general

It is quite probable that you will have more than one priority debt. Any surplus you have should be concentrated on these areas. It is a good idea to start negotiating with the 'smallest' priority creditor or the one that is most likely to agree to your proposals.

As you negotiate with your creditors keep a record of all your dealings with them – make notes of telephone conversations and keep copies of all letters you write and receive. When agreement has been reached write to them confirming your agreement. You should then add these figures to your financial statement so that they become part of your budget. It is also worth writing to your other priority creditors to let them know about the agreements you have received. This may make them reconsider and accept proposals they had previously rejected. When you have reached agreement with all priority creditors you can use any balance to repay your other debts.

If you do not even have enough surplus income to repay your priority debts then you need to look again at your financial statement. If your creditors know you are really trying and going without things such as new clothes in an effort to repay them they might just treat you as a special case and accept smaller repayments over a longer period of time.

In conclusion, you need to protect your home, your warmth and your liberty. Generally, your priority creditors do not need to knock on your door to get paid. People who do this, or who constantly phone you, are rarely chasing priority debts. They are trying to get in first because they know they cannot resort to the sanctions available to priority creditors. Some, especially if debt collectors or money lenders are involved, do not care whether you lose your home or your warmth, they are only interested in being paid.

Remember: it is important to reach agreement on settling your priority debts first. Only when you have done this should you turn to your other debts and see if there is a way to pay them off as well. This is what we will look at in the next chapter.

ACTION PLAN

1 **Communicate with your other priority creditors. Have you, where appropriate, written to the relevant offices about: (a) gas, (b) electricity, (c) water, (d) Council Tax, (e), ground rent, (f) maintenance, (g) telephone, (h) tax?**

eight

Low Priority Debts

This brief chapter looks at your unsecured creditors. These are lower in priority than your secured creditors because they pose less of a threat to you: they cannot immediately threaten your home or possessions.

Unsecured, low priority creditors include credit cards, store cards, catalogues, personal loans, hire purchase agreements and so on. To recover their money they have to sue you through the courts, but remember that the court can be your friend as well. If you can reach agreement before going to court obviously it is for the good.

Just like dealing with your priority debts you need to gather certain information as follows:

- Copies of all agreements signed.
- Total amount you owe, including arrears.
- Rate of interest being charged.
- Are there, or could there be, any extras charged, such as on cancellation?
- Is it a *revolving credit account* (see chapter 4 for details) and if so what amount of interest is being charged each month?
- Are there any insurance policies taken out that cover redundancy or sickness?

An example of such a letter is given on the next page:

Date   Your address

Creditor's address

Dear Sir,

(Enter your account number here – this can be found
on your last bill)

I would be grateful if you could send me the following
information as soon as possible:

1 The total amount outstanding on the above
  account.
2 Are there any interest or service charges being
  added to the account and if so how much?
3 Does the account cover a fixed term or is there a
  revolving credit agreement?

I am afraid I have mislaid my original copy of this
agreement and I would therefore be grateful if you
could send me a copy. As soon as I have all the above
information I will write to you again.

  Yours faithfully
  (Your name)

At this stage it is a good idea to return any store or credit
cards with the letter, making sure they are cut in half.
This should help prevent further debts mounting, as well
as making it more likely, if you eventually ask, for interest
to be frozen. A recent survey indicated that people spend
34% more if they have credit cards. They seem so
convenient at the time, but . . . !

When your creditors have replied you will first need to examine the copies of the agreements to ensure they are correct. If an agreement was entered into after 19 May 1985 it must include the following information:

• The names of the lender and borrower
• The price of the goods and a description of them
• Credit limits
• Rate of interest (APR)
• The total cost of the item, including credit
• When payments are due

If for some reason your agreement does not contain all this information then you should seek legal advice because you might be able to challenge your creditor. Other points worth remembering are that the lender has to be licensed under the Consumer Credit Act 1974, and that you have to be at least eighteen before your signature can be legally binding. It is also possible to apply to the court to alter the terms of the agreement, especially if you feel you are being charged an extortionate rate of interest. Sadly, your view of what is extortionate may well differ from the court's, but it is possible that in certain circumstances you will be given more time to pay.

In most cases, however, the agreement will be legally complete. It therefore becomes necessary to enter all relevant information received from the creditors on to your financial statement. It is at this stage that negotiation with your non-priority creditors begins.

ACTION PLAN

Communicate with your other creditors where there is a lower priority to pay.

nine

Negotiating with Creditors

It is important to bear in mind that in most cases the creditor will want to negotiate a solution with you. If your situation has changed for the worse most creditors will be sympathetic and will try and make adjustments for it. This is partly because of genuine concern and partly because any adverse publicity could be particularly damaging.

If you find that your creditors are responding with concern it is important to recognize some guidelines for your negotiations:

1 **Treat your creditors with respect.** It is important that you try to separate the person from what he is telling you. In other words, it is important to remember that you may well be dealing with someone who is just doing his job and who has in effect been told what to say. *So stay polite.* However, this does not mean that you have to accept or agree with everything that is said.

2 **Try to stay calm.** There are bound to be tensions when you are trying to negotiate. You may well feel that you have been talked into certain situations which went beyond your better judgement. Even if this is the case it will do you no good whatsoever if you start criticizing and arguing with the creditor. It is only likely to make things worse.

3 **Acknowledge the creditor's limitations.** It is important to recognize that your creditor's representative

is probably going to be working within certain constraints. These can be because of the nature of the organization or because of his position in it. For example, a branch manager may well feel that in your case a period of three months' suspended payments is the best for all concerned, but if proposing that is outside his remit or is not company policy he simply will not be able to propose it. It is, therefore, important to try and establish whether the person you are dealing with is operating within such constraints. This is of course a powerful reason for dealing with the most senior person you can find.

4 Point out benefits to creditors. There could be a considerable number of times when you may be able to make suggestions which would actually be mutually beneficial. To take an extreme example, if a building society had gained a possession order through the court and was planning to repossess and then sell the property, it could well be of benefit to you both if you stayed and tried to ensure a sale with you in it. This would be beneficial to you as you would be in your home for some time longer and would give you breathing space to make alternative arrangements. Equally, the building society is likely to get a higher price with lower costs attached if you stay and sell the property – even if they are getting no mortgage payments in the meantime.

5 Try to set and stick to limits. It is important that you have a definite plan which you try and stick to. You may want to try to clear all your debts within a certain space of time. On the other hand you may not want to pay more than a certain amount off each month, because otherwise you would be facing real hardship. Whatever you do, stick to your position and make sure you do not succumb to pressure and pay an awkward creditor more than others.

These strategies should be fine for most creditors, but there may be some who remain unhelpful, angry and

abusive. Different tactics need to be employed here. If the
creditor is demanding large payments, rather than make
offers you cannot afford to pay, start by suggesting a very
low figure. Later on in the negotiations you can 'give in'
and raise your figure to a level that you would have offered
a more sympathetic creditor in the first place. Another
strategy would be to try and let them see that you have
every sympathy with them and would do more if only you
could. For example, if they are berating government policy
share the frustration you have faced in this area. By doing
this sympathy may increase to such an extent that a
compromise may after all be found! If all else fails and you
have produced an accurate financial statement, ask them to
show you how you can increase your offer without being
unfair to other creditors. By concentrating on the factual
rather than the emotional a solution may be found much
more quickly.

As you start to get responses from creditors expect some
tried and tested attempts to persuade you to pay more.
These can include:

1 *'You have a good income.'* Provided your financial
statement is accurate you can soon get rid of this one. If
your income is 'good' you can quickly point out that sadly
you have expenditure and debts to match! You should have
no problem here as long as your proposals are equitable.
2 *'You are spending too much.'* This again can best be
countered by an honest financial statement, but there will
need to be an explanation given for the points raised.
Therefore, if the size of the phone bill is queried and you
can point out that the majority of the cost is related to your
job, you can answer the point satisfactorily. The item
which undoubtedly causes the most contention here is
cigarettes. These can always be included in the 'food and
household items' box. However, if they are questioned the

reality of your addiction and inability to overcome it (including attempts to do so) should be clearly stated. My own somewhat limited experience does indicate that an above average number of people in debt do smoke, but I think it can safely be argued that it is the stress of debt causing people to smoke more, rather than the cost of the cigarettes causing the debt. Perhaps someone should do a thesis on the subject.

3 *'We are not a charity.'* Often creditors will present a 'pseudo-sympathetic' face: 'We would love to help and be generous, but we are in business and if we accepted all proposals we would soon be in major difficulties ourselves.' The answer to this is to stress that you are not in fact looking for charity. What you are doing is putting forward a business-like proposal based on the new circumstances in which you find yourself. The accompanying financial statement showing, where appropriate, the changes in your circumstances should help achieve this.

4 *'Look at all the mistakes you've made!'* Many of you will fit into this category because mistakes are so easy to make. Some of you may have delayed too long in first getting in touch with your creditors. Others may have taken out new loans to repay old debts. But whatever the circumstances it is essential to emphasize here that you have changed. Any financial advice you have been receiving, copies of an accurate financial statement and even evidence that you have been reading this book should help here!

5 *'Everybody else is paying.'* Firstly, this is unlikely to be true. Secondly, it really does not matter what everyone else is doing. If you are offering the maximum you can afford there is no more that you can do.

6 *'It can't be done.'* Creditors will sometimes argue that their system cannot cope with reduced payments. As it has probably picked up that you have made no payments for some time, however, it could perhaps be a bit too selective!

All you can do is repeat your offer as the best you can achieve.

7 *'We'll do it if you increase the security.'* Some creditors may agree to your offer of reduced payments on condition that you offer them some form of security, usually your home. This is known as a 'voluntary charge' as it converts an unsecured loan into a secured one, and means that once the property is sold the debt should, in theory, be paid in full. This is a complete non-starter as you are increasing your risks enormously.

8 *'We'll keep charging you interest.'* Any repayment offer should be conditional upon the cancellation of any future interest charges. The creditor may accept your reduced offer on condition that you are still charged interest. This would be unfair on other creditors who had accepted your offer unconditionally. It would also give little incentive to you if, for example, you could only afford £10 a month and the interest you were being charged was £15 per month.

Bearing in mind the above it is now important to draw up a revised financial statement allowing for payments that you have agreed with priority creditors. After these adjustments you may or may not have a small surplus which can be allocated to non-priority creditors.

If you have a surplus

If you have a surplus the first thing you need to do is add up all the non-priority debts. Then you divide your surplus income in proportion to the amount of each debt. This is how it is done:

Individual debt × surplus income ÷ total debt = offer

If you are as mathematically astute as I am this may leave

you holding the page to the light! Hopefully an example will make this easier.

Assume you have a surplus of £50 a month and your four debts are:

- Credit Card   £ 500
- Bank Loan   £ 750
- Store Card   £ 250
- Family Loan   £ 100

  TOTAL   £1600

Using the formula above you can make a fair offer to each of your four non-priority creditors on a pro-rata basis. For example, the credit card payment would work out like this:

$$500 \text{ (individual debt)} \times 50 \text{ (monthly surplus)}$$
$$\div\ 1600 \text{ (total debt)} = \text{£}15.62 \text{ (monthly offer)}$$

By using this formula for each of the four debts your repayment picture would look like this:

- Credit Card   £15.62
- Bank Loan   £23.44
- Store Card   £ 7.81
- Family Loan   £ 3.13

  Total monthly repayment   £50.00

In the above example you can also work out that it would take you 32 months to repay all the debts (£1600÷£50 = 32 months).

This system ensures that each creditor receives a fair

percentage of your surplus income. When you are dealing with a revolving credit account (such as a credit or store card) it is important to get them to cancel any future interest charges. Do not make an offer without making it clear that the freezing of interest is part of that offer.

Creditors will quite often feel that they would rather have a regular monthly payment, even if at a lower level, than spasmodic payments of varying amounts or nothing at all. It is much less costly administratively and there is, therefore, a reasonable chance that you will reach agreement. If they refuse they will end up having to sue you through the courts, at which time you will be able to explain your offer clearly.

Having worked out the payments you can make you now need to write to your creditors. A letter to a fixed term creditor (such as a bank loan) should be along the following lines:

Date   Your address

Creditor's address

Dear Sir,

(Enter your account number here – this can be found on your last bill)

I am now enclosing a copy of my current financial statement showing my present income and expenditure, including what I am paying on my priority debt arrears.

Since I started this agreement my circumstances have changed significantly and I now find that my surplus income figure is only £ (enter your surplus income figure). I intend to divide this surplus fairly and in proportion to the debts shown on the enclosed list.

I hope that this is acceptable to you. Could you please confirm this so that I can start making these payments to you.

Yours faithfully
(Your name)

If you are writing regarding a revolving credit account however (such as a credit card) you need to say a bit more and write as follows:

Date   Your address

Creditor's address

Dear Sir,

(Enter your account number here – this can be found on your last bill)

I am now enclosing a copy of my current financial statement showing my present income and expenditure, including what I am paying on my priority debt arrears.

Since I started this agreement my circumstances have changed significantly and I now find that my surplus income figure is only £ (enter your surplus income figure). I intend to divide this surplus fairly

and in proportion to the debts shown on the enclosed
list.

Unfortunately, the amount that I can afford to offer
you does not cover/barely covers the present accruing
interest. Since I can only afford this amount if I am
not going to be unfair to my other creditors would
you please agree to freeze the account and suspend
further interest to enable me to clear the debt?

I look forward to your reply and hope that my offer
is acceptable to you so that payments may begin as
soon as possible.

Yours faithfully
(Your name)

Together with these letters you will need to send a revised
copy of your financial statement showing your priority debt
payments as well as a list of your priority debts. Remember
to treat all non-priority debts in the same way however
much pressure you are put under. And never negotiate
over the phone – apart from the cost, you need written
confirmation of any offer and the responses.

Having written it is likely that you will get various
responses from creditors. Some may feel that you are
trying to see just how much you can get away with. Others
may not believe that you will keep to your agreement –
especially if you have a bad payment record. All you can do
is persevere and convince them that you mean what you
say.

Once the replies arrive you need to look at their
response and act accordingly. You will find yourself in one
of the following categories:

1 *All the creditors agree to your offer.* If this is the case –
congratulations! Start making the agreed payments right

away. If your circumstances change for the better during this period, increase your payments and it will mean you will get rid of your debts that much faster. If, on the other hand, things get worse let your creditors know immediately.

2 *All the creditors refuse your offer.* If this happens, don't give up. Take another look at your financial statement. Have you really trimmed it back as far as you can? If you believe you have then you can expect eventually to appear in court. They will decide whether your offer is fair.

3 *Most creditors refuse your offer.* In these circumstances it is a good idea to ask them why they have refused. This will make them look again at your case. They may argue that a specific item you are paying for is not essential. You will need either to sell the offending item and adjust your offer, or argue convincingly as to why you need it. In the meantime you need to start to pay those creditors who have accepted your offer.

4 *Most creditors accept your offer.* If most creditors do accept, immediately write to the others and tell them so. The creditor could well reconsider when he sees that he is in a minority. The letter should be along the following lines:

Date   Your address

Creditor's address

Dear Sir,

(Enter your account number here – this can be found on your last bill)

Thank you for your letter of [enter date of their letter] concerning the above account.

I am sorry that you are unable to accept my offer. (Nearly) all of my other creditors have accepted similar terms and I have started paying them. I cannot offer you any more because I am unable to afford more and I need to be fair to all my creditors.

Given that the other creditors have agreed to accept the reduced payments I have offered I wonder if you would be good enough to reconsider your decision.

I look forward to your reply.

Yours faithfully

(Your name)

Whatever you do, do not offer a difficult creditor more money. This is not only unfair to those who have already accepted your offer, but it throws your honesty into question.

What do you do if a creditor refuses to accept your offer?

In some cases, even after reconsideration, creditors will not accept your revised offer. They may, for example, refuse to suspend interest, which they are legally entitled to do. This could mean that your monthly offer would not even match the monthly interest accruing. If this is the case you need to ask them to reconsider their position in order to give you some incentive to pay. The letter should be in the following form:

Date   Your address

Creditor's address

Dear Sir,

(Enter your account number here – this can be found on your last bill)

Thank you for your letter of [date of their letter] regarding the above account. I am sorry that you feel unable to suspend interest charged on my account. My offer has been accepted by most of my creditors and I have started to pay them accordingly. I am not in a position to increase my offer to you.

Since I opened this account I have already paid considerable sums of interest and even if you did agree to suspend interest from this time it will still take me (your figure) months to pay off this debt unless my situation improves significantly.

If you look at my financial statement again I think you will agree that I cannot afford any more and on that basis, and bearing in mind the reaction of the other creditors, I would ask you to reconsider.

Yours faithfully
(Your name)

If at the end of the day your creditor refuses to accept your offer you will have to invite him to take you to court. This could mean that you end up on a credit black list, but it could still be to your advantage to go to court. You should write as follows:

Date   Your address

Creditor's address

Dear Sir,

(Enter your account number here – this can be found
on your last bill)

Thank you for your letter of [date of their letter]. I am
very disappointed that we have been unable to reach
an agreement in this case. The offer I have made to
you, and which you have rejected, cannot be
increased. What is more you are still insisting on
charging me interest and it therefore seems pointless
to make any further payments while my debt is still
increasing every month.

   Reluctantly, I think that the only solution is for you
to sue me for the debt. In court I will make the same
offer that I have made to you as I believe it to be the
fairest I can make in the present circumstances. I
believe that once the court has made its judgement
you will be unable to charge any further interest.
Going to court will involve us both in extra time and
costs, but there would appear to be no other solution
unless you are prepared to accept my current offer.

   If you agreed to suspend interest and accepted my
offer I would begin paying immediately.

   Yours faithfully
   (Your name)

It is always worth reminding a creditor that once a judgement is made interest cannot be charged on the account.

Remember, whatever their reactions, keep your creditors informed and be polite. Keep your letter short and to the point, but ensure that they are fully aware of your relevant circumstances. If you are finding it hard or nerve-wracking to negotiate, ask someone else to help you. Your local CAB or a debt counsellor would be a good place to start. Often a letter from someone 'official' will persuade a creditor that you are genuine or at least that you are taking professional advice.

Do not have anything to do with anyone who offers to help you in return for a fee. They could end up as yet another creditor on the list.

If you are unable to pay

If there is no surplus income to pay to non-priority creditors you will need to write to inform them of the situation. There are several options worth exploring here:

1 *A complete or partial write-off.* If you have no available income or capital and you can see no immediate improvement likely, then you can ask for a debt to be written off. If they agree, you no longer have to carry the stress of the debt and can start again. In certain circumstances the creditor may be able to offset any loss against tax. However, creditors rarely just write off debts. They may decide to take no further action on it, which could leave you worrying for years that they will suddenly start chasing you for it. Equally, they are likely to tell a credit reference agency, which will keep details of this on their records thus making it hard for you to get credit again in the future.

A partial write-off reduces the debt to a level where you have a chance of paying something. This will give you the incentive to pay as you will be able to see an end in sight. Certainly a partial write-off is more helpful to an unsecured creditor than bankruptcy, where he may well end up with nothing.

It is important to ensure that interest is frozen on all your non-priority debts. You will then know that every time you make a payment your debt is reducing and will eventually be cleared. This should nearly always be used with other options, as in the example below:

Date   Your address

Their address

Dear Sir,

(Enter your account number here – this can be found on your last bill)

Please find enclosed a copy of my financial statement which shows my present monthly income and expenditure. It is clear from looking at it that after essential payments such as my mortgage there is nothing remaining with which to pay your account.

Given the above, would you please suspend all interest charges and at the same time accept nil payments until my circumstances improve. I am doing all I can to increase my income and as soon as I achieve something I will let you know.

I am also writing to my other creditors with the same request. Thank you for your attention and I look forward to hearing from you.

Yours faithfully
(Your name)

Offering a capital sum in full settlement

You may be in a position where you have no surplus income but you do have some saleable assets, in which case an offer of a smaller lump sum for early settlement might well appeal to a creditor. For example, if you were able to sell your stamp collection for £5,000 and had debts of £10,000 you could offer each creditor 50% of what you owed. You would be able to clear your debts, and the creditors may well feel this is the best opportunity they are going to get.

But whatever you do it will only work if you are truthful with your creditors and stick to any concessionary agreements you have made. If your circumstances change, contact all your creditors immediately.

ACTION PLAN

1 Negotiate with all your creditors in a respectable and responsible manner.
2 Be aware of the various objections they have, and have answers ready for them.
3 Work our how much to offer creditors if you have a surplus.
4 Be able to respond to your creditors regardless of how they reply to your letters.

ten

Going to Court

A general overview of the present court system will help us to understand which court deals with which type of case. Basically there are two different types of case.

Firstly there are criminal cases. These are initially heard in the magistrates' court, but if necessary a full trial is heard in the crown court. Then, again if required, there is the court of appeal (criminal division) and ultimately the House of Lords for a final decision.

Secondly there are civil cases. These cases are generally brought about because different people or organizations have a dispute. In most cases the first court in the civil court system is the county court. Occasionally the high court or magistrates' court would be more appropriate. In the case of an appeal there is the high court, the court of appeal (civil division) and again the House of Lords – whichever is appropriate.

Where debt is concerned it is usually dealt with by the civil court system.

The high court will deal with large debts, especially if they are over £50,000. It will also deal with smaller debts if the case is referred to it by the county court, especially if the debt is above £25,000 and seems to be particularly complicated.

The county court *must* deal with all debts regulated under the Consumer Credit Act, as well as all claims under £25,000. In addition most debts for gas, electricity, water rates, mortgage arrears, tax and National Insurance arrears, credit card debts, unpaid bank loans, over-payment of benefits and other money debts will be dealt with in the county court.

The magistrates' court will deal with unpaid fines, council tax arrears, unpaid maintenance and VAT arrears.

If the debt is for £1,000 or less then it could well be settled using the small claims procedure. This process is held in private and is quite informal. First of all the plaintiff gets to explain his version of events and then the defendant can explain his version. There will also be the opportunity for each side to question the other side. When it is your turn to speak it is important to have prepared what you want to say. Be precise and stick to the facts. The judge does not want to hear your life history but he does want to hear *both* sides of the argument. The judge may then further question both sides before making his decision. He will normally decide there and then. The judge will *not* have decided in advance. Generally speaking he will have only seen and read the papers a few minutes before the hearing.

As part of the government's Citizens' Charter there is now a Courts' Charter. This explains about the standard of service which you can hope to expect from the people who work in courts. Court staff have to wear name badges, they have to be courteous and generally efficient. The Charter also explains how you can complain, although this does *not* include the opportunity to claim for compensation for any mistakes. The court will write to you outlining any mistake it has made and the steps it is taking to avoid a repetition. When you receive your court papers you will also get details of how to find the court (including a map) and details of where you can park nearby.

I will now concentrate on the county court and start with the events leading up to a court appearance. To make the process easier to understand, a hypothetical case of a credit card debt of £2,000 has been used. The example is typical of how the majority of money claims are settled.

The County Court – Default Actions

There are three types of action that a creditor can take in the county court. Initially the focus will be on *Default Actions*, which are used to recover money – in our example a credit card debt. There are also *Fixed Date Actions* to recover goods; and *Possession Actions* to recover property. These will be looked at later.

Before court proceedings begin on the hypothetical debt, Mr Spender will receive a warning letter called a *Default Notice*. This states that if he does not pay the £2,000 immediately then court proceedings will commence. Obviously Mr Spender cannot pay the £2,000 because he has spent all his money. So he ignores the letter and probably two or three subsequent letters as well. He hopes that the problem will simply go away. Therefore the Easicredit Finance Company finally lose patience and request a *Default Summons* from the court. It is worth pointing out at this stage that it is still not too late to negotiate a repayment schedule. Some companies threaten court action to try and generate a response but do not always intend to carry out their threat. However, the Easicredit Finance Company does decide to take action.

The court having considered the request from the Easicredit Finance Company will then serve a *County Court Summons*, usually by first class post, and this is done on form N1. The court assumes that Mr Spender will have received his summons seven days after posting and therefore considers that it has been served. This applies even if Mr Spender claims that he hasn't actually received the summons!! Sadly, it is very common for people like Mr Spender to claim that they haven't received the summons, so the courts will ignore him and issue a *Judgement in Default* anyway. This means that Mr Spender has to put forward a very good argument in order for the court to consider setting the judgement aside.

So, Mr Spender has received his summons (N1) and with that there will be several other forms. There will be a form with the particulars of the claim (although this might be on the summons if there is room) and two forms of reply. They are forms N9A (admission) and N9B (defence and counterclaim). We are concerned with N9A because Mr Spender does not dispute that he owes the money. However, he could respond in several other ways. He could admit owing only part of the claim, deny that he owes any money at all or make a counterclaim.

Before moving on it is important to give a word of warning. Whilst preparing this book I managed to talk to a District Judge who said the following:

> *'Incredible as it seems, over 50 per cent of all cases are decided in default because people don't bother to fill in the court forms.'*

The courts are there to be fair to both sides. They are generally very sympathetic to people who have fallen on hard times, especially in these days of recession. The courts will often 'bend over backwards' to help if only people would communicate with them!

If you get nothing else from this book please learn this lesson:

Fill in all court forms and, if required, turn up for the hearing. It can, and probably will, save you much heartache!!

To continue with Mr Spender, he has now received all the

above-mentioned forms. He has fourteen days to reply, although he could ask the Easicredit Finance Company to extend the period. If they agree to this request then he *must* get confirmation *in writing* from them – a verbal agreement is not good enough.

Mr Spender therefore fills in form N9A (admission) and returns the form *to the plaintiff* rather than to the court. The forms are quite simple to complete and you should not be frightened of them. It is very important to keep a copy of the form, and it would also be wise to get proof of posting from the post office. This then eliminates the possibility of the Easicredit Finance Company claiming that Mr Spender didn't reply to the summons and therefore claiming a Judgement in Default. You will see the importance of this later. As well as admitting the claim, Mr Spender has to make an offer to repay the money owing. His offer will be based on his financial statement, which has already been explained in detail in Chapter 4, and this will probably be on a pro-rata basis depending on his disposable income and his other creditors.

At this stage the Easicredit Finance Company has two options: they can accept the offer or they can refuse it.

If they agree with the offer then the next thing Mr Spender will receive is a *Court Order* stating when, where and how much he has to pay. This is called *Entering Judgement on Admission*. Money should *not* be sent to the court. If this sequence of events occurs then you will notice that Mr Spender does not attend court at all and this in itself is a good enough reason for filling in the forms.

If the Easicredit Finance Company disagrees with the offer then it has to make a very careful decision. If the offer is fair, depending on the individual person's circumstances, then the court will consider that the amount of money offered is fair and will judge accordingly. The court would not be impressed with the Easicredit Finance

Company if it pushed Mr Spender too far, and this could affect future cases involving them. Most plaintiffs would contact Mr Spender to discuss the matter, but they have to be very careful not to pressure or harass him into making an unrealistic offer. If both parties cannot agree then the plaintiff will complete a form outlining the reasons why they object to the offer and how much they would be willing to accept. This form is then returned to the court, along with Mr Spender's offer.

A court official will then look at both sides of the argument and follow court guidelines before deciding how much should be paid. These guidelines are linked with Mr Spender's ability to pay. If the official agrees with either Mr Spender's offer or the Easicredit Finance Company's objections then he will enter a *Judgement by Disposal* and make an order. Both sides will get a copy of the order which will state how much, where, and when is to be paid. Again no money has to be sent to court and again you will notice that Mr Spender has *not* had to attend court.

It is perfectly possible, however, for the court to agree with the plaintiff and issue a judgement that Mr Spender feels he cannot afford. He therefore has fourteen days to appeal on form N244 (obtainable from the court) or by writing a letter to the court. He has to explain why he thinks the judgement is unfair and must enclose any relevant papers, together with his up-to-date financial statement. This is particularly important if his circumstances have changed since the onset of court proceedings. Mr Spender must then attend a hearing (for the first time) when the district judge will consider the appeal. If the judge agrees with Mr Spender he will change the order and send details of the new payments to both sides. If the court does not agree then it will still contact both sides and restate the original order.

Once the judgement is entered, the Easicredit Finance

Company can take legal steps to *enforce* the order if Mr Spender fails to keep up with the payments. We will look at how to enforce judgements later. If Mr Spender had not replied to the summons then a Judgement by Default would have been made and *payment forthwith* demanded. This means that *the whole* of the debt becomes due *immediately* and if it is *not* paid then enforcement can take place straight away. If this happens it is vital that you apply to the court to *set aside* the judgement or *vary the order*. The court will only set aside a judgement if there are good reason for doing so – for example, if you can prove that you did not receive the court papers. The court may also vary the order if you can argue that you cannot afford the repayment. If the judgement is set aside it will be cancelled. If this situation applies to you it is vital that you seek expert advice as soon as possible. Legal Aid may be available.

In addition to the plaintiff being able to enforce the judgement for non-payment there are other consequences for Mr Spender. His name will be registered in the Registry of County Court Judgements and this will make it difficult for him to obtain future credit. The details will be kept on file for six years. If the debt is paid *in full* within one month of entry then he can apply to have it removed. If he pays the debt *after* one month then the entry is not removed but amended to show that he has a County Court Judgement (CCJ) and also that he has paid it.

If Mr Spender admitted only part of the claim then that part will be judged as above and the disputed amount will be settled in court. If he disputed all of the claim then it would all be settled by the court. If Mr Spender had disputed the claim and lost he would *not* be registered in the CCJ register unless he then asked for time to pay the debt.

At any time before a hearing the case can be settled out

of court and this will probably reduce costs. If you admit only part of a claim then you are also allowed to make a payment into the court *on account*. This can have the effect of reducing costs if you win the disputed amount. If you are thinking of making a payment into court then you should seek advice first.

Fixed date actions

Following on from looking at Default Actions you will remember that in order to take action for the return of goods a Fixed Date Action is required. When a *Fixed Date Summons* has been served, again together with forms N9A and N9B, there will be a hearing, which usually takes place six to eight weeks after the summons. The date for the hearing might well be on the summons. If *both* sides agree then a letter can be sent to the court to *adjourn* the hearing. The hearing can also be adjourned if there are other reasonable grounds, for example if you have to attend hospital for an operation on the same day. If only *one* side agrees to an adjournment then a letter can be sent to the court detailing reasons why you want an adjournment and stating the case reference number. There is also a court form (N244) which can be used. You would need to send a copy of your letter to both the court and the other side, preferably by *recorded delivery*.

Nowadays, if you dispute the action and wish to enter a defence there is a procedure called *Automatic Directions*. This means that, unless the judge feels it is helpful, you do not need to attend a pre-trial review. This review is to discuss how the court will deal with the case. It is now a fairly standard procedure and therefore the court will send both sides some guidance notes. The notes explain the actions that both sides have to take and how long they have in which to carry out these actions.

If the court has not already set a date for the hearing it

will do so after the defendant returns his N9A or N9B or when sending the automatic directions. As before, it is very important to check that the date of the hearing is acceptable and if not to contact the other side as previously outlined. Also check that you know where the court is.

On the day of the hearing it is recommended that you arrive early, as this allows time to find out which court your case is in. There is usually a list pinned up, but if not you should ask the court usher or the clerk of the court. In any case it is wise to give your name to the usher, who will probably be wearing a gown, so that he knows you have arrived. The usher will point out where to sit while you wait for your case to come up, which can take several hours. This means that it is better not to take your children with you.

If the claim is for less than £5,000 then it will probably be dealt with by a district judge. The district judge should be addressed as 'sir' or 'madam'. It is recommended that you dress smartly. Try to avoid arguing and try to be tactful. Think before you speak and never be afraid to ask for advice if you do not understand a question or you are unsure of what to do next. As already stated, prepare what you want to say. Start at the beginning, stay calm, stick to the facts and give the judge time to make notes. Keep your eyes on him and only start speaking again when he has finished writing. You will probably be nervous and therefore it is important to concentrate on the proceedings. Listen carefully and take your time if you are struggling to find the right words. It is important that you are not aggressive or abusive, whatever the provocation. It will certainly not help and might in fact lead to further trouble.

If you attend a small claims hearing you may have the right for a *lay person* to help you to present your case. This person could be a law centre volunteer, a Citizens' Advice

Bureau worker, a friend or anybody else. You should check with the court to see if this is allowed.

In most instances the only people in court will be those connected with the case. When both parties have presented their side of the argument then the judge will make his decision. Occasionally he will *reserve judgement* to a later date and will fix another date for his decision. The *plaintiff* can ask the court for an *oral examination* of the *defendant*'s financial position. This means that you will be asked very searching questions about your finances, and will have to sign to the effect that the answers you have given are true. After the court has reached its decision it can make one, or a combination, of the following orders. It can award compensation, the return of property, the repayment of money owed (either in instalments or as a lump sum) or one of several orders which we will be looking at later. You cannot appeal against a decision made in the small claims court but you can appeal if the case was heard in the full court. You need to seek legal advice if you are thinking of making an appeal, and legal aid may be available.

We will now take a look at the third of the three types of action, namely possession actions.

Possession actions

If you are unable to reach agreement with your mortgage lender then you can expect to receive a *possession summons*. This is on form N5, and it tells you that you are being taken to court and also when the hearing is. As well as the summons there will be a particulars of claim form. This will detail the mortgage agreement and the amount owing. There will be a form to reply to the summons (N11) and you have fourteen days to reply to it. Again, as with all our previous examples, you need to make an offer to repay the arrears and your financial statement should form the basis of that offer. The N11 form asks if you are willing to give up your home and also asks if you agree that the lender has the right to take possession. *You should always answer NO!* This is because you may need to apply to the local authority for rented accommodation at some time in the future and they will class you as having made yourself *intentionally* homeless unless you do answer in this way.

Because it is to everyone's advantage to try and sell the property with you living in it, you should still try to negotiate with the lender even after possession proceedings have begun. You should ask the lender to suspend or adjourn court proceedings for a period of time, say three or six months, and during that time make an agreed payment. For people on Income Support the new Payment Direct system has been a triumph. The mortgage interest is paid direct to the lender after sixteen weeks of claiming benefit, and although you might get into arrears in the first sixteen-week period when only half the mortgage interest is paid, you should not get into further trouble. However, this can be seen as a double-edged sword because there is very little incentive to take a low-paid job as this would mean losing *automatic* entitlement to this benefit.

It is absolutely vital that you turn up at the court. You are allowed to take a friend or adviser with you.

Do not ignore the summons!

If you do not attend then the court will make an order against you anyway and you could lose your home. It is important to turn up even if you have reached agreement with your lender. The court hearing will *not* be held in public and will probably be very short. The court is not especially interested in how you got into the arrears but is more concerned about how you intend to repay the debt.

It is therefore important that you furnish the court with an up-to-date financial statement together with your proposals. As before it is important to prepare what you want to say and then stick to the facts.

If you can show that you can pay off the arrears straight away *and* keep up with future payments the court will probably dismiss the whole thing. If the court feels that you can catch up fairly quickly it might adjourn the matter for, say, six months and then review the matter. The court might grant an *outright possession order* if it feels that you have no chance of paying off the arrears. The most common decision is called a *suspended possession order*. This decision is made when the court feels that you can pay off the arrears over a reasonable time scale *and* keep up with future payments. The definition of 'reasonable' is almost impossible to define. Some courts will say two years while some say three. It is not uncommon for some to say five years and I have even heard of one court that granted someone seven years, although I cannot substantiate that as a fact.

The suspended possession order states how much you have to pay and how often. If you keep up with the payments then the lender cannot evict you. As with all our previous examples, we will be looking at what happens when you do not or cannot keep up with the payments later.

Even if the court grants an outright possession order it is still not too late to save your home. The order states a date when you have to leave your home and that date is normally 28 or 56 days later. If you do not leave on that day then the lender has to apply to the court for a *possession warrant*. The lender can *not* evict you without this warrant. This process takes time and you should keep trying to negotiate with the lender. This might stop the lender from applying for a warrant and will also give you more time to find alternative accommodation.

Before the final eviction takes place the bailiffs will probably visit to tell you when they plan to act. They will try to find out if the eviction will cause any problems, for example with elderly or sick residents. Even at this stage it is still possible to apply to the court for a *suspended possession warrant*. This might be relevant if you are able to make a new improved offer to pay or if you need more time to sell the property or more time to find another home. If you apply for the warrant to be suspended you *must* attend the new hearing.

It is never too late to apply for a suspension of a warrant, even if you are due to be evicted on that very day.

If you are unable to put off the fateful day then you will be evicted on the date specified by the bailiffs. The bailiffs' powers will be discussed in the next chapter. Somebody representing the lender will be there to receive the house from the bailiff, and locks will be changed to stop re-entry. Even if you are not there you will still be evicted. The house must be vacant and therefore you will need to remove your possessions. If you don't, they will be removed for you.

Even after you have been evicted you are still responsible for the mortgage until the house has been sold. If the price the house fetches is not enough to repay the debt then you will still be liable for the outstanding amount. This outstanding amount will now become a non-secured debt and is therefore no longer a priority debt. If you have mortgage indemnity insurance this *does not* cover you but rather the lender, and therefore the indemnifier will try to recover the debt from you. If you are unhappy with the way your lender has acted during your difficulties then you should complain, firstly to the lender direct and, if necessary, to the relevant ombudsman.

Variation orders

The three main types of action that a creditor can take against you have now been covered. If you have had a judgement entered against you with a *payment by instalments* order then it is absolutely vital that you keep up the payments as directed by the court. If you do keep up the payments then you will not lose your home, your possessions or even your liberty. However, if you do not keep up the payments then your creditor can *enforce* the judgement in the court. This can result in you losing your home, your possessions and even your liberty, depending on the type of debt, and depending on the type of order that the creditor and the court decide on. We will be looking at these options shortly, but first of all we will discuss a very important option open to the person in debt.

This option is known as a *variation order*. If you realize that you are unable to keep up with the payments – perhaps because of a fall in income or some other circumstance – then you can apply to the court for a reduction in the payments. This is done on form N245 (obtainable from the court), which includes space for writing down your financial details. When the court receives your details they will follow certain guidelines to determine how much you should pay. If you are unhappy with the court's decision you can appeal to the district judge for a final decision. If your circumstances change again then you can apply for a variation order again. There is no limit to the number of times you can apply for a variation order, provided that your circumstances have indeed changed.

If the payment is reduced and you keep up with the new payments then the creditor is still not able to enforce the debt. This is because you have not broken the court order.

**Please try and remember the following:
If you cannot afford the payments then apply for a
variation order. Do not miss payments!**

There are other alternatives that you may be able to take.
These options are available only in certain circumstances.
You will need to read about all the alternatives before
deciding on a possible plan of action. The first of these is a
time order.

Time orders

Time orders are a relatively under-used and apparently
complicated option. Even some courts are unsure of how
they work and therefore tend to follow their own customs
and practice. Some courts will even refuse to consider time
orders at all. So what is a time order?

A time order is a request for more time to pay a credit
debt. You can only take this option when you have received
a *default notice* from the creditor and the credit is regulated
under the Consumer Credit Act. A time order can be
applied to both secured and unsecured loans but normally
you would try to agree a repayment schedule with an
unsecured creditor rather than apply for a time order. If
negotiations fail it might be appropriate to apply for a time
order, especially if you want to avoid having a County
Court Judgement (CCJ) entered against you.

You can apply for a time order as soon as you receive the
default notice. You need to use form N440 and a fee of
£40 is charged. In some circumstances it may be possible
to ask for the fee to be waived if you cannot afford to
pay it. The second way of applying is after legal action
has started. This will probably be when a creditor is
threatening repossession of your home or perhaps a car.

This is done on a different form (N244) and there is no charge.

If you have applied for a time order you must attend the court hearing. If you apply on form N440 then you will not be registered on the CCJ register, but if you apply on form N244 you run the risk of judgement being entered anyway. In other words, form N244 will not prevent a CCJ and the subsequent entry on the register. This is obviously important because you would then find it difficult to obtain credit in the future.

So why are time orders so complicated?

The district judge has several options open to him. Firstly he can reduce the interest rate if he considers that the interest being charged is extortionate. However, it is very difficult to quantify extortionate. The current mortgage base rate can be compared with creit card rates of over twice that much and some store card rates in excess of four times! This means that there is no definition of extortionate but it could be relevant in your particular case.

If you apply for a time order and claim that you are being charged an extortionate rate of interest, you can expect some very severe opposition from the creditor. He will probably employ a barrister to fight your application. This is because the judge might reduce the interest rate and this could have severe repercussions for the business – if everybody applied to reduce the interest rate then the company would lose a fortune. By reducing the interest rate the judge is fundamentally changing the original contract. Therefore if you do apply for a time order and the creditor does employ a barrister you might have to pay his very high costs. Some judges are now telling creditors that although they are entitled to employ a barrister they will not automatically be awarded costs, particularly if the interest rate is not the main point of the order.

Alternatively the judge can allow you to repay the debt

by reduced payments, suspend interest altogether or make any other change he feels is appropriate to your case. The major problem is this. Some courts decide that the time order can only be applied to the amount of arrears accrued rather than the whole debt. This means that you still have the problem of repaying the normal monthly amount in addition to your arrears payment. Some courts, however, will make a time order for the arrears as well as the rest of the outstanding loan.

As a result of all the controversy, many courts are refusing to consider time orders. As the debt crisis worsens and more people become aware of this option, time orders will probably become more and more common. There needs to be some common standards adopted so that everybody will know whether a time order is the right option to take. In the meantime you will need to seek advice as to the viewpoint of your own local court.

Administration orders

An *administration order* means that you are allowed to make a single monthly payment into the court and the court will pay your creditors on a pro-rata basis for you. The court charges a fee for doing this work and it is currently 5%, i.e. for every pound you pay 5p goes to the court and 95p goes towards paying off your debts. In theory administration orders are a good thing, but there are circumstances that must apply in order for you to qualify for one. Also, as with other options, there are advantages and disadvantages to administration orders.

In order to apply for an administration order you need to have the following – at least one county court judgement outstanding, not more than £5,000 of non-priority debts, and money owing to at least one non-priority creditor.

Priority creditors are not generally included in administration orders because they have other ways of getting their money back and therefore would probably be unhappy at limiting their own powers. There are plans to do away with the £5,000 limit in the near future, but as I write the limit still applies. Before considering an administration order it is best to have negotiated with your priority creditors for repayment of their debts. Some priority creditors, for example the gas or electricity boards, might agree to be included on an administration order but they would also retain the right to disconnect your services.

There is no uniformity in how the courts decide which debts to include for the purposes of adding up total debts. Some include priority debts in the total, but not in the order. Some courts include the whole mortgage, which just about disqualifies all owner-occupiers from applying. This is why it is important that the £5,000 limit is either raised considerably or scrapped altogether. If your debts are more than the limit then you could ask your creditors to write off some of the debt to bring you below the £5,000 limit. You are advised to seek help from the Citizens' Advice Bureau or other similar organization if you are considering an administration order.

So what are the advantages of an administration order?

You only make one payment into the court each month and the amount is based on your ability to pay. This means that you have a certain amount of peace of mind. There is no further interest added to the debt once the order is made, although this does not apply to High Court debts. Once the order is passed all other County Court actions are stopped. This is particularly important if you have several creditors threatening court action at the same time. It also avoids the problems of court forms, visits from bailiffs or court appearances and the extra costs all of this entails. The courts can make what is called a *composition order*, which means you only pay a percentage of the debt. The court is effectively writing off part of the debt. Some courts will make a composition order even when you don't apply for one! Applying for an administration order can also stop a creditor from making you bankrupt if they don't apply within twenty-eight days of being informed of your intentions to include them in the order. This applies if the debt is for £1,500 or less.

The disadvantages of an administration order include the following:

- The current £5,000 limit disqualifies a lot of people with large debts.
- There is no time limit to an administration order and therefore you have to pay the debt in full (unless a composition order is made). This could take a very long time, whereas if you elected for bankruptcy the debt is generally cancelled after three years.
- The court's fee of 5% of the debt has to be paid as well.
- The monthly payment can be reviewed if either the court or the creditor applies for a review.
- You are not allowed to obtain credit of more than £10 without informing the lender.
- Legal aid is not available at the hearing but you may be able to get help with filling in all the forms. There may well be a free legal clinic in your area or again ask at an advice bureau.
- You will also be disqualified from holding certain posts and offices.
- Finally a lot of judges will only grant an administration order if it is with an *attachment of earnings order* (more later). This means that your employer would have to know about your debts and this could also have serious consequences depending on your type of job. You would be forced to apply for a *suspended attachment of earnings*

order to prevent your employer from finding out. This would probably be granted. You are effectively asking the courts to trust you to pay on time. If you missed payments then the order would come into force.

An administration order is administered by the Chief Clerk of the court and it is automatically reviewed every three months. The court staff now have the authority in some circumstances to make, revoke or alter administration orders without the need for a court hearing or even the need to involve the judge. All administration orders will now be entered on the CCJ register. As previously stated, an administration order has no set time limit but in practice ten years is generally considered as a maximum. It is worth applying for a composition order if your normal monthly payments would take longer than three years to repay the debts. When you apply to the court, using form N92, there is a section relating to 'x pence in the pound'. An example of how to work this out should make the point clear.

Suppose you owed £4,500 (including court costs) and you could afford £30 per month. If you multiply £30 by 36 months you would pay £1,080 in total. As a proportion of the total outstanding this can be calculated as follows:

$$\frac{1080 \times 100}{4500} = 24\%$$

Therefore you would write on the form 'or to the extent of 24 pence in the pound'. If you were old, a single parent, disabled, ill or unlikely to become a high wage earner you would have the best chance of being granted a composition order but each court tends to follow its own policy.

If a creditor is accidentally forgotten then the court can decide to add them to the administration order. After the order is made a listed creditor is entitled to ask the court to seize and sell any of your property valued at more than £50. In practice this is almost never done.

The district judge has the discretion to allow or refuse an administration order. If the judge considers that the debts have been taken on wilfully he is more likely to refuse. Again, if you have some valuable possessions that you are refusing to sell to reduce the debt he is more likely to refuse. Finally you can apply to the court to vary the order if your circumstances change. If you consistently miss payments or miss two consecutive months then the court will tell you of its intention to *revoke the order*. You must reply within sixteen days.

An administration order only finishes when the total debts, or a percentage if relevant, *plus* the court costs have been paid.

ACTION PLAN

1 **Be aware of how important it is to fill in all court forms and attend all hearings.**
2 **Be aware of the various actions/forms that you could come across.**
3 **Don't be frightened by the thought of appearing in court – it can often help you!**

eleven

The Courts –
Bankruptcies and Bailiffs

Individual voluntary agreements

An *individual voluntary arrangement*, hereafter called an IVA, could almost be described as a legal way of negotiating with your creditors. In order to do this you need to enlist the services of an independent person called an *insolvency practitioner* (IP), who is generally a solicitor or an accountant. The IP generally prepares and monitors an offer to pay your creditors, usually non-priority, and gets paid for doing this. He must be authorized and your local court should have details of whom to contact.

Anybody who realizes they are in serious financial difficulty can approach an insolvency practitioner or could be referred to one by the court. Sometimes people go to one when a creditor threatens to make them bankrupt, and you can even approach him after a bankruptcy order has been made. You can go to him regardless of the amount of debts or assets that you have.

A court might refer somebody to an insolvency practitioner when that person has voluntarily asked to be made bankrupt. Generally this would be if the person has debts of less than £20,000 and assets of at least £2,000, provided that the person concerned has not previously been made bankrupt or entered into an IVA within the past five years. It is up to the court to decide to cancel a bankruptcy order if someone approaches an IP after bankruptcy.

If you have trouble contacting an IP then you should approach the following:

The Insolvency Service of the Department of Trade and Industry (071 215 5000) if you live in England, Scotland or Wales, or The Insolvency Service, Lindsay House, 8–14 Callender Street, Belfast BT1 5DU (0232 248885) if you live in Northern Ireland.

An insolvency practitioner does not work for nothing. The fees charged can be very high, and if possible you should compare several prices before agreeing to someone's services. Legal Aid is *not* available and so the fees have to be included with the other creditors as part of the final arrangement. However, the creditors will only receive their money when the insolvency practitioner has been paid. An IVA is not always the best course of action for somebody with a large debt problem, and therefore it might be worth asking an IP if he or she would grant you an initial interview to discuss the options at a reduced cost or even for free.

If your income means that you can afford regular payments and you want to sort out your debt problem with your creditors, then an IVA may be a good step to take. This becomes more relevant if you want to try and save your family home or business – or indeed both!

There are obviously both advantages and disadvantages with an IVA and some of the more obvious ones are mentioned here.

Advantages
If you have a profitable business then a creditor is likely to allow you to continue in order that you can pay back more of your debt. This means that you may be able to keep your home and business and therefore lose less than if you were

made bankrupt. Additionally, the stigma of being made bankrupt, even though it is now more common, and the ensuing newspaper publicity, can be avoided. The costs involved, although expensive, may still be less than those in a bankruptcy. The whole scheme can be designed to maximize each individual's assets and limit possible liabilities. Finally, some of the consequences of bankruptcy are avoided.

Disadvantages

When someone is declared bankrupt they are automatically discharged after two or three years. An IVA can often last longer than this period, but some judges nowadays are limiting IVAs to the same period and writing off some of the debts. The judge will often state that he doesn't see why somebody should be 'penalized' for taking advantage of an IVA. It will probably take more time to work out the practicalities of an IVA with an insolvency practitioner than it would with the trustees of a bankrupt person. Secured and preferential creditors will still have to be paid in full unless they agree otherwise. Finally, you may be prevented from carrying out your work (e.g. solicitor or lawyer) or from taking up certain posts or offices.

The actual mechanics of applying for an IVA are dependent on each individual person's circumstances and are obviously beyond the scope of this book. If you need further help then please seek specialist advice.

Bankruptcy

Bankruptcy is a word that seems to provoke feelings of failure and despair for many people and has led to suicide and countless emotional breakdowns. Unfortunately, in today's economic climate it is becoming more and more common and seems to be regarded as one of the pitfalls of a modern society. Many people, however, have little idea of what is involved.

Bankruptcy is a legal process that may benefit a person who cannot pay his debts. A trustee ensures that all the available assets are distributed amongst the creditors and this process usually goes on for two or three years. At the end of that time most, if not all, of the debts are written off and the person concerned can make a fresh start.

A creditor can apply to make you bankrupt or you can apply to make yourself bankrupt. Bankruptcy is an individual choice and therefore couples must *each* apply. In certain circumstances a joint application for bankruptcy can be made if the debts are business debts and all partners agree. This does not apply to limited companies. As with all the other options discussed, there are advantages and disadvantages to bankruptcy.

Advantages

Once you have been made bankrupt your creditors will have to deal with your trustee and this will obviously reduce stress, strain and pressure. As already mentioned, you will probably be discharged from your bankruptcy after two or three years and this means you can make a fresh start. Apart from certain debts such as court fines, secured loans, maintenance payments and one or two other debts (which might also be written off) most of the money that you owe will be written off. However, you would still need to assist the trustee with the remaining debts. Finally, you would still be able to carry on with your chosen trade or profession in most cases – exceptions are listed below.

Disadvantages

You will not be able to do certain jobs or hold public office. Examples include being a company director (unless the court agrees), an MP, an accountant, a solicitor, an estate agent, a local councillor, a school governor or a trustee of a charity. You will also lose your major assets, which could include your home and your business. This could also mean having to make people unemployed and some of these people will probably have become family friends. Additionally, you will have to close any bank or building society accounts, hand over life insurance policies, credit cards, etc., and if you refuse to co-operate you could get into further trouble with the court. The trustee now has a legal obligation to tell the electricity, gas, water and telephone companies about you. The company will then probably treat you as a new customer and ask for a guarantor before opening a new account. The whole bankruptcy procedure is expensive and time-consuming, and your personal details will end up in the newspapers. You could also be publicly questioned about your financial affairs. When the bankruptcy is discharged you may still struggle to get credit, buy a house, or perhaps start a new business. As already stated, some of the debts might not be written off. If a bankrupt person was to inherit some money then that could also be confiscated by the trustee. Finally, there are certain things that are classed as criminal offences if a bankrupt person does them. Examples include obtaining credit or starting another business, lying about your financial affairs, leaving the country with goods worth more than £500, and many others.

Bankruptcy would be an option for somebody with no assets, living in rented housing and an employee. For many other people it is an unthinkable last resort that is to be avoided at all costs. It goes without saying that anybody being threatened with bankruptcy or contemplating voluntary bankruptcy should seek specialist advice as soon as possible. This could be from their local Citizens' Advice Bureau, Credit Action (0223 324034) or perhaps from The Bankruptcy Association of Great Britain and Ireland (0524 64305 or 0482 658701) which is a relatively new organization set up to combat the growing problem, particularly concerning businesses.

Enforcement options

Having looked at many options that are available to
somebody in debt it is now time to look at the options
available to the creditor if the debtor does not pay.
Remember, this applies to repayment specified by the
court at the time of the County Court Judgement (CCJ).
As long as you keep up with your payments then the
creditor cannot enforce the judgement. If you are
struggling to keep up the payments then you should always
apply for a variation order, and therefore there is really no
excuse for getting to this stage. However, as already said, a
lot of people simply ignore the problem and so disqualify
themselves from all the previous options. Quite obviously
the creditor runs out of patience and decides to ask the
court to enforce the debt. One of the ways, as has already
been seen, is to threaten bankruptcy (or indeed carry out
the threat).

Other options available to the creditor include *oral
examination* to see whether it is worthwhile trying to
enforce the judgement. Assuming that they do wish to
proceed with enforcement, they may have four main
options to consider. Depending on the type of debt one or
more of these options may be relevant.

1 *Seizure of Goods.* The creditor applies to the court for an
order called either a *warrant of delivery* or a *warrant of
execution.* The latter allows bailiffs to enter your home to
seize and sell possessions to the value of the debt. If the
judgement was for HP goods then they can reclaim the
creditor's property, specifically with a warrant of delivery.
Remember that HP goods are not yours until you have
made the final payment.

2 *Attachment of Earnings Order.* The court orders that the
monthly repayment is taken directly out of your wages.
Your employer will charge you £1 per deduction to help
with administrative costs. If you refuse to tell the creditor

who you work for then they will probably ask the court to carry out an *oral examination* which will also add to the debt. The court sends you a form (N56) which you have to return within 8 days. This asks for details of your finances and your employer's details. Sometimes the court will go direct to your employer for details of your pay, especially if you do not return the N56 form. If you don't fill in the form then the bailiffs will serve a *statement of means* form for you to complete. If you refuse to fill that in then you will have to attend a hearing before the court. If you don't turn up for the hearing the court will issue a warrant to bring you before the court or even to send you to prison! When you complete N56 you will also be able to apply for a *suspended attachment of earnings order* which means that the court will not deduct money from your wages provided you pay what the court decides. This could be very important because some employers will dismiss employees because they don't like all the problems of administering orders. The court will not make an attachment of earnings order if your take-home pay is low. The low figure is known as the *protected earnings rate* (PER) and is dependent on each person's circumstances. Very roughly the PER is in line with what you would receive if you were on state benefits.

If you have an attachment of earnings order and you then get other CCJs you can ask the court for a *consolidated attachment of earnings order*. If you do not mind having money deducted from your wages this can be to your advantage. As there is only one deduction there is only one charge. The court and your employer make the payments to the different creditors for you, so there is less work for you to do. If you need to vary the payments then they are all varied at the same time. The order will lapse if you become unemployed. If you change employers then you need to tell the court of your new employer's details. You should always tell the court if your circumstances change.

3 *Charging Order.* This effectively turns an unsecured loan into a secured loan. This does not mean that you will lose your home but it means that you cannot sell your home without paying your creditor. This type of order can apply to property jointly owned by you and somebody else. Once a *charging order* has been made the creditor can apply to the court for an order forcing the debtor to sell. The courts will only grant this request in a few rare cases. If the home is mortgaged then the charging order only applies to the equity after the mortgage is paid off. Some creditors, in particular banks, will ask you to make a *voluntary charging order* on your home. It is considered to be better to have a charging order rather than to agree to a voluntary one because the court will be the administrator rather than the creditor. It is vital to seek legal advice as soon as you are told that somebody has applied for a charging order.

4 *Garnishee Orders.* This type of order forces someone who has money, for example in a bank or building society, to pay a creditor straight away. It is usually made against self-employed people or for business debts. The creditor normally gets details of your finances through an Oral Examination. This type of order is very rarely used against personal credit debts. There is nothing to stop you removing money from a bank account if you suspect that somebody is applying for a *garnishee order*. The order only applies to the money in the account on the actual day of the order. A garnishee order has two distinct stages. First of all a *garnishee order nisi* (*nisi* means 'unless') is made by the court when the creditor applies to it. This freezes the debtor's bank account until the matter is sorted out. If you wish to fight against the order then you need to get legal advice urgently. In the vast majority of cases a *garnishee order absolute* is granted and the money is paid to the creditor in a lump sum.

I was told of a striking example of this method of

enforcement and I will relay the tale to you now. A man
went shopping one weekend and bought a cheap electrical
appliance from a very well-known high street store. When
he reached home and tried to use the appliance it was
faulty and therefore he returned to the store for a
replacement. To cut a long story short, the store refused to
replace the item. Therefore the man, with typical British
determination, decided to sue them through the small
claims court. The man duly won his case and the store was
ordered to repay him plus his court costs. Several weeks
elapsed and there was no sign of the man's money. After
seeking advice he applied for, and was granted, a
Garnishee Order Nisi and the whole bank account for this
multi-national company was frozen! Needless to say the
man was paid his money *within one hour!!!* The point of this
story is this: the courts are there to help both the little man
and the massive multinational companies.

In conclusion, it is never too late to try and negotiate
with a creditor, but if the creditor thinks that he will be
paid in full in the near future then he is very unlikely to
agree to any repayment programme.

Bailiffs

A bailiff is a person who carries out evictions, enforces
money debts and injunctions and repossesses goods.
There are four different types of bailiff and they perform
different duties.

County Court Bailiffs are employed by the Lord Chan-
cellor's Department to enforce county court judgements.
This is usually for amounts under £5,000; or to repossess
goods regulated under the Consumer Credit Act.

Sheriff's Officers are bailiffs who enforce High Court
judgements. They are independent of, but responsible to,
the court.

Private Bailiffs are employed by most local authorities to enforce Community Charge or Council Tax arrears. Private bailiffs can also be employed by the Inland Revenue, HM Customs and Excise to collect VAT arrears, or even by the court to collect fines. In all these case the private bailiff is responsible to the body concerned, and these bodies will lay down guidance procedures for the bailiff to follow. Anybody can become a private bailiff.

Certified Bailiffs are granted a certificate by the county court which means that they have certain powers. The certified bailiff has to apply to the court every two years to have the certificate renewed. The government bodies already mentioned are more likely to employ a certified bailiff than a private bailiff, because the certified bailiff will have satisfied the court that he is a fit and proper person with a sufficient knowledge of the law to carry out the duties required.

The county court bailiff who is responsible for enforcing debts of £5,000 or less is the one you are most likely to meet.

The bailiff will have received a *warrant* or a *writ* giving him authority to carry out the instructions on it. Warrants are issued by the county or magistrates court, whereas a writ is issued by the high court. The warrant or writ will usually give the bailiff the power to seize goods or property. When the bailiff seizes goods he must give you a *notice of distress* which informs you that goods have been seized. In order to seize goods the bailiff must have made a peaceful entry into your home. It is not enough to post the notice of distress through the letter box, and bailiffs cannot *usually* make a forcible entry into your home.

Once the warrant has been issued it is still possible to negotiate. This can be done direct with the bailiff or with the creditor. You can also apply to the court to have the warrant or writ suspended. When you get to this stage time is of the essence because the bailiff will insist on your signing a *walking possession agreement*. What this means is that rather than removing your goods they will be left in your home for a further five days provided you do not get rid of them. If a private bailiff is being used you will be charged a daily fee which is added to the debt. The bailiff will then return to remove the goods at a later date unless you have either paid the debt and charges in full, had the warrant suspended or successfully agreed a repayment schedule. In practice a bailiff will not remove your goods straight away although they are legally entitled to. Once you have signed a *walking possession agreement* then the bailiff can return at any time and can use force to gain entry. If the bailiff thinks that things could turn nasty he will enlist the help of the police who will stand by in case of a breach of the peace. If you refuse to sign a walking possession agreement then the bailiff can issue a *close possession agreement*. This means that somebody will stay and guard the goods. This option is extremely rare and is more likely to happen where goods of high value are involved. If you do not agree to a close possession agreement either then the bailiff will remove the goods straight away.

In order to apply to the court for a *suspension of a warrant* you again need to use the form N245. The courts will decide if the offer is reasonable and therefore may suspend the warrant. It is possible to suspend this more than once, but eventually the court will decide that enough is enough.

So what is it that a bailiff is and is not allowed to do?

The bailiff can arrive at any time to try and seize goods. In practice the bailiff will give you seven days' notice about the visit. This obviously does not apply if they think you will try to get rid of your goods before they arrive. Bailiffs do have the right to enter your home but they have to do so peacefully. Therefore they cannot get in by breaking a window or door, opening a window that is not already partly opened, barging their way in when you answer the knock at the door if you do not want them to enter, or knocking down gates and fences. However, they can get in by climbing through an open window, opening a door or window that is partly open, opening a door that is closed but not locked, climbing over a neighbour's wall or even opening a lock by reaching through an open window. Once the bailiff is in he can break down internal doors and break open locked cupboards or drawers. He can also break into other buildings not connected to the main house, for example a garage or garden shed. If you allow a bailiff to trick his way in for example because he says he just wants to give you some forms or just wants to discuss the matter, then it is too late. He will be in and then he is able to carry out his duties. Remember that once you have signed a walking possession agreement the bailiff *can force entry*.

If the bailiff cannot get into your home he will probably try again or report back to the court that he cannot gain entry. He may also be able to seize goods from business premises or from the home of a third party if he suspects that they are looking after your possessions.

Bailiffs can seize goods but not permanent fixtures. A shelf will be considered as goods but fitted wardrobes would be treated as fixtures. A cooker would be treated as goods even though the pipes and fittings are fixtures. If there are no goods to seize then the bailiff must leave immediately, otherwise he becomes a trespasser.

Finally, the bailiffs cannot seize clothing, bedding, furniture, equipment, and provisions which are necessary for the basic needs of you and your family. In addition tools of your trade to the value of £50, books, vehicles and equipment needed to carry out your employment cannot be taken. This can be interpreted in many different ways and only really applies to county court bailiffs. Private bailiffs could look at these guidelines differently. As in all cases already mentioned, it is vital to seek further help and advice. Court bailiffs are doing a job like anybody else and are generally extremely helpful. They are dealing with this type of thing every day and therefore provide a good source of advice. Private bailiffs are paid by results and are less inclined to be helpful. They might tell you that you *have* to negotiate with them. This is simply not true and you are advised to keep trying to negotiate with the creditor as well.

ACTION PLAN

1 Get to grips with the advantages and disadvantages of bankruptcy.
2 Recognize the various enforcement options that can be brought against you.
3 Familiarize yourself with what bailiffs can and cannot do.

twelve

The Special Problems of Redundancy

Redundancy can strike anyone at any time. During the recession of the early 1990s 25 per cent of the UK workforce has experienced unemployment, and of those half are home owners. So if it has happened to you remember you are neither to blame nor alone. Given that, if you are in this category, you may have turned immediately to this chapter I will cover some areas briefly as they have been given more space earlier in the book.

1 Examine your situation at work

Employees have a few rights when it comes to redundancy, and employers have to carry out redundancies in a fair way. Firstly, employers must try to minimize redundancies, for example, by reducing overtime payments to others or reducing the number of temporary staff they employ. Where possible retraining should be offered. If redundancy looks inevitable, however, you should have been informed about it at the earliest opportunity.

You then need to look at your contract. The length of notice you receive will depend on it. You could be paid in lieu of notice and asked to leave straight away. Whatever you do do not give in your notice and leave of your own accord because you think you are going to lose your job. In these circumstances you would not be able to claim redundancy pay. If on the other hand you feel you have been selected unfairly you can complain to the Advisory Conciliation and Arbitration Service (ACAS). Employers need to consider such things as length of service, experience, conduct and attendance records when making their decisions, so if you really do feel you have been singled out for unfair treatment let them know.

Your employer has a variety of other options open. You could be offered alternative employment, for example. If you don't take it then you forfeit the right to redundancy pay. If the job is unsuitable after at least a month's trial you can then ask to take the redundancy. Your employer may also ask whether there are any employees who wish to take either voluntary redundancy or early retirement. If you volunteer for redundancy you will not lose your entitlement to redundancy pay, provided you do not leave before being made redundant. If you are near retirement age you might be offered early retirement instead of redundancy. This can be a good option if you think you will struggle to get another job, as you may well be able to draw pension benefits early.

You can try and negotiate with your employer. See whether you can keep your company car or try to get outplacement or financial counselling at no cost to yourself.

2 Statutory redundancy pay – your minimum entitlement
Check the terms and conditions of your contract of employment to ensure that your minimum pay-off terms agree with it. Statutory redundancy pay is the legal minimum payment for employees who have been made redundant. You must have been in full-time work for two years and be at least twenty to qualify. If you are a part-time worker you need to have been working there for at least five years. The payment is worked out on the length of service with your employer. Certain other factors complicate the scene. These include your age, the fact that you are deemed not to be able to work more than twenty years with one company and that there is a maximum weekly wage figure used in the calculation.

3 Severance and ex-gratia pay

Many employers have schemes which offer more than the
statutory minimum. Your contract will show whether you
are eligible. Others may well decide to make 'one-off'
payments which are over and above any legal or contractual
payments to which you may be entitled. They may be made
as a thank you or because of special circumstances and are
sometimes referred to as golden handshakes.

4 Tax

Redundancy payments are tax-free up to a limit of
£30,000. Anything above this has to have Pay As You Earn
(PAYE) deducted by your employer before it can be paid to
you. If you fall into this category it would be tax-efficient to
pay the excess into your company pension up to the
allowable limit if you can afford to do so. Another thing
that would help previously high wage earners is to be
made redundant at the beginning of a new tax year. This is
because tax could be paid at only the basic rate. Things
don't usually work out like this though!

5 Explore the benefits system

Many of you will have been working since you left school
or university and will therefore have very little knowledge
of how the system works. When you leave work you should
be given a P45 form with your final wage payment. It is
important that you sign on at the local Unemployment
Benefit Office the first working day after you leave your
job. This is not only to ensure that you get unemployment
benefit as soon as possible, but also because your national
insurance contributions will be paid for you once you sign
on. This can be quite demeaning and usually involves lots
of queuing, waiting around and eventually lots of paper
work.

Your entitlement to Unemployment Benefit depends on

your National Insurance contributions over the past two years. You can claim even if you have received a large redundancy settlement, but if you resigned voluntarily or were dismissed for misconduct you will not be paid for the first six months. More details of this and items like the other possible benefits to which you might be entitled are covered in the chapter on communication.

6 Budgeting

A redundancy payment is paid in part as compensation for loss of future income. As soon as you know what income you will receive in terms of redundancy pay and benefits you should start to draw up your budget. Again you need to refer to the chapter on budgeting to get the hang of this, but here are some basic points which could be of particular help to you if you have just lost your job:

a It is important to contact all real and potential creditors. Explaining your situation and keeping in regular touch with them really is the best thing you can do. They are aware of the pressures unemployment brings and in most cases will do everything they can to help as long as they are convinced you are being open and honest.

b If you have a mortgage ask your lender if they will be prepared to accept lower, or interest only, payments while you are unemployed. Most will probably be happy to try and help as long as you let them know right away so there is no chance of any arrears building up.

c If on the other hand you rent a property you may be able to defer payment – especially from the council. Again, discuss the situation straight away.

d Remember in the above two cases that if you have limited assets (under £8,000) you will probably be eligible for help with your housing payments either through Income Support or Housing Benefit.

e Pay as many bills as you can by means of a monthly budget account. The more accurate your budget is the less likely you are to be hit with an unexpectedly large bill which could do so much damage.

f Remember, your fuel and lighting bills will soar if you lose your job and stay at home when the house would otherwise be empty – especially in winter. Even spending some of that time at the local library would cut those costs considerably.

g With lower priority debts (such as credit cards) only make offers when you have reached agreement with your priority creditors. Obviously keeping a roof over your head is your first priority.

h Economize, working through the budget, whenever you can.

i Contact your tax office and see if any rebates are due to you.

7 Housing

It is important to consider the various options you have. Could you sell your home and raise sufficient capital to give you a useful nest egg if you moved to somewhere smaller or another part of the country where property is cheaper? Can you use some of your redundancy money to reduce your mortgage to a more affordable figure? Do you need to change the type of mortgage you have? Are there endowment policies currently covering the mortgage which have real value if they are sold? Look in detail at the chapter on housing to see how this really could affect you.

8 Reduce debts

If you have been given a lump sum do not invest it at 5% interest if you are being charged 25% interest on some debts! Try and clear off the most expensive things first – the unwanted overdraft, the store cards and credit cards. Try and avoid using credit whilst income is tight.

9 Insurance

Many of you at work will have been provided with life and medical insurance by your employer. Before you leave see if your company is prepared to offer an extension on your membership of these schemes while you are looking for another job. This could both save you money and give you protection for an extra time. If not, it is worth taking out basic life cover.

10 Pensions

Basically, if you are in a company scheme the options are to leave it where it is or transfer it to a personal pension. Another thing would be to wait until you have a new job and then transfer from the old scheme to the new one.

Do not rush into any decision. If you have just been made redundant your life is likely to be in turmoil anyway. Firstly ask your employer what the transfer value of the pension is, and then check what the benefits are for leaving the pension with the company either frozen or deferred. If you have been in employment with the company for less than five years you may have to take it with you anyway.

11 Investing the lump sum pay-off

Again it is important not to be rushed. Until you have a clear idea of your future plans put any lump sum redundancy into a high interest instant access account. Do not tie up any of your money for a long period of time until you are certain that you will not need it immediately. It is a good idea to take solid independent advice in all the areas of insurance, pensions and investments.

12 Acknowledge your emotions

It really is important that anyone who is facing unemployment or redundancy should read the chapter on emotions. Redundancy causes major disruptions to your life and is usually stressful. Many have compared it with bereavement, as you not only lose your sense of worth and your income but often there are many friends you will find it very hard to keep in touch with. Again the key points are:

a Acknowledge your feelings and talk them through with family and friends. Although they too will have worries about it they can be a source of great support. Be honest with your partner however much it hurts – it can only get worse if you bottle things up and keep quiet.

b Try and make contact with others who have been through the same thing by meeting them through Job Clubs or the like.

c Expect to feel some (or all) of the following:
   - **shock** – expressed by denial of the problem, 'busyness', apathy, lack of sleep
   - **depression** – bitterness and hopelessness
   - **acknowledgement** – realistic acceptance of the problems and the possible solutions
   - **adaptation** – beginning to plan for the future, taking positive steps and thus becoming less anxious

The progress of this pattern will obviously depend on your character and situation. If depression sets in don't be afraid to go to your doctor.

13 Plan your time

It may be difficult but try to establish a pattern, with sensible meals and time for looking for work and relaxation.

14 Looking for a job

It is a good idea to start looking for a new job as soon as you know you are going to be made redundant. All sorts of factors come into play when you look for a new position – your skills, qualifications, experience, age, location and the local employment rate are all important factors to consider. Also of importance are the quality and quantity of your job applications. You could sometimes be fortunate enough to be the right person in the right place at the right time.

The first thing you need to do when looking for a job is to draw up your CV. CV means *curriculum vitae* which literally means (I am told) 'the course of your life'. Your CV should be short and factual, emphasizing what you can offer to a potential employer. You should be prepared to talk about all or any part of your CV if you are called for an interview. The CV needs to be laid out clearly and should include the following information:

- **personal details** – name, address, telephone number, date of birth
- **family details** – husband/wife, children
- **work experience** – start with your most recent position and state your job title, main responsibilities, company name and nature of their business
- **your education** – include all qualifications
- **other useful skills** – driving licence, languages, etc.
- **your interests** – to give a potential employer a broader picture of what you are like as a person

It takes time to produce a good CV. The importance of a good one can be gauged by the fact that there are now many people who prepare CVs for other people as a business. So present your CV attractively and make sure all the facts are put across clearly. If you have responsibilities in a non-work situation or have done temporary or voluntary work, include details as this can only increase your chances of being seen for an interview. See sample below:

Sample CV

Personal Details:
Name: J. Smith
Address: Neighbours, 1 Coronation Street, Newton
Telephone: 0123 45678
Date of Birth: 1.2.60
Marital Status: Married, 3 children
Nationality: British

Career Objective:
Having worked as a senior draughtsman for six years I am now
seeking a managerial position in an engineering firm or similar
establishment which will give me scope to develop my managerial
skills.

Work History:
1986–present   Senior Draughtsman with HighTec
                Engineering, Ramsey Street, Newton. My
                duties include assistance with research and
                design, quality control, and supervision of
                work on major projects. I am in charge of a
                group of twelve skilled workers.

1980–86   Draughtsman, Seethrough Designs,
                Emmerdale. I worked on a wide variety of
                design projects, and received further training in
                advanced design, including a full accreditation
                in the Institute of Technical Design.

Qualifications:
1978–80   Newton Technical College
                City and Guilds certificate in Technical
                Drawing.

1974–78   Newton Comprehensive School
                CSE English, Maths, Technical Drawing,
                Physics, Woodwork, History, Geography,
                Needlework.
                I received a school prize for Technical
                Drawing.

Leisure Interests:
                Football, athletics (Secretary of Emmerdale
                Athletics Club) and computing.

Referees: Available on request.

Similarly, if you are filling in an application form the first thing that will be noticed about it is the appearance. It is the first impression that your potential new employer has of you – and you may be literally one of hundreds of applicants. So try and fill in the forms accurately and neatly. It is well worth writing out some of the more detailed parts in rough and then only filling in the form when you are happy you have got all the points across clearly.

When writing to potential employers always enclose a copy of your CV with the application form if you have been sent one. There are many places to look for jobs – Job Clubs, vacancy boards, employment agencies, and advertisements in national and local newspapers and on radio. In addition there is nothing to stop you writing to other employers in your area if you believe that your skills would fit into their organization. It is also important that you keep your ear close to the ground. Social contacts are very important. After all, they know *you*, not your CV. Listen to hear whether your friends know of any job opportunities there may be for you. Seek their advice.

Before following up any vacancy try to plan your approach. Think about what is needed to do the job well and then consider whether you have the necessary skills to do just that. Try and find out as much about the company as you can. This should impress if you reach the stage of being called for an interview. Keep a copy of all the applications you make, and keep the advertisements as well so that you can remember the key things the employer is looking for should you be selected for interview.

If you are unemployed and you haven't had an interview for a long time it is a good idea to brush up on your interview technique. This can be done either with a friend or with the help of someone from your local Job Club. In the interview try and look confident. You are obviously trying to make a good impression so say why you think you could do the job – but don't appear brash! Ask questions about the company to show you are interested in them. Be prepared to talk about the fact that you were made redundant. Explain that there was nothing wrong with you or your work, it was just the economic circumstances or whatever. Try very hard not to appear desperate or negative as this will undoubtedly count against you.

15 Advancing your situation

One positive aspect that redundancy brings is that it can provide the opportunity, the time and the cash to do something new. Perhaps you have always wanted to start your own business or work from home. You may even have wanted to move somewhere entirely new. Before you rush off and do so it is important to weigh up the risk. Do you have all the necessary skills or do you need further training before commencing your new enterprise? Do you have enough cash, including your redundancy payment, to make it financially viable? Are the rest of your family in agreement with your decision? There will be many questions as well, so try and get as much information and guidance as you can. Talk to career advisers and others who are already doing similar work.

If you are thinking of moving or of opening up a small business somewhere make sure you thoroughly check the property situation. If you are thinking of taking a course make sure you have the necessary qualifications. You may well be eligible for a grant. It is well worth asking what percentage of previous course applicants got a job at the end of it. There can be little worse than to go through weeks and weeks of hard work only to find your employments prospects are no better at the end.

It is especially important, if you are thinking of using your lump sum redundancy payment to open up your own business, that you take professional advice. Most new businesses fail not because what they are doing is unnecessary or unwanted. It is because they are either undercapitalized or fail to understand the need for a steady cash flow. You can be the best electrician in the world but without appropriate business skills you may still not survive financially. Remember too that with the capital outlay it will probably be some time before the company comes into profit. Your local Job Centre should be able to put you in contact with government-sponsored agencies that provide all the necessary advice. The Enterprise Scheme may be able to provide some form of financial assistance if you are thinking of starting up on your own. Your local Training and Enterprise Council will also be able to help.

A visit to the local business unit of your bank could also be of value. They are well used to helping people set up in business and will almost certainly have a lot of literature that will be of much use to you. They may also offer you a period of cheap banking to help you establish your business.

I know what it is like to be made redundant, with the fear and pain it usually brings. I only hope that the points raised in this chapter will in some way help you cope with it better, and that all of you will feel that you have not been written off for ever just because you have been made redundant. Whatever you are looking for – whether it's a new job, starting up your own business or having more leisure time – I hope you find it. Whichever category you fall into you will probably have to watch the pennies carefully for some time, so this next chapter could be useful to you as well.

ACTION PLAN

1 Ensure you receive your minimum redundancy
  entitlement.
2 Ensure you are getting all the benefits to which
  you are entitled.
3 Start to live by a budget.
4 Acknowledge that you will probably be coping with
  emotions similar to those felt in bereavement.
5 Do all you can to get yourself another job.

thirteen

Living Without Debt

The way to clear your debts, or even avoid them in the first place, may be quite straightforward if you are able to raise the money. On the other hand you could face several years of living frugally before they are all behind you. Whichever category you are in you need to look at the reasons why you got into debt. The most probable ones are:

- you lost your job
- you over-committed yourself financially, with either too big a mortgage or too much spending with credit cards
- you were persuaded by advertising pressure to take on more commitments than you could afford
- you had never been taught how to handle your money responsibly

Whatever the reason your aim should be to prevent a build-up of debt ever happening again. It is important to remember that there will be all sorts of family and personal pressures while you are trying to sort out your debt situation. Money will be very tight and this is bound to lead to an increase in stress. This is a perfectly normal reaction and it is important to recognize that these sort of tensions will occur. Don't be afraid of seeking counselling or going to the doctor during these difficult times.

There are also quite a few things that you yourself can do practically that will help you avoid debt or at least speed your getting out of it. The list below is by no means complete but it should contain some points that each one of you should find useful. It should, therefore, help reduce the stress and pain that debt can cause. Not all these ideas will work for everybody, and I apologize in advance if any sound patronizing. My wife has made it very clear to me, for example, that she believes any attempt that I might have at making my own clothes would soon lead our family into debt! It would, therefore, not be a good idea for me, however much it might amuse the rest of them. Seriously though, talking through this list with your family may well produce ideas that could be fun as well as money-saving. Why not work through the following and put a tick beside any suggestion you think would work for you? You could then sit down and plan together how you can practically put your ideas into action.

1 Only buy on a cash basis. If you can't afford something, save up for it.

2 When you are thinking of buying something ask yourself whether it is something you or your family really *need* or whether it is something you just *want*. Remember, tomorrow's needs are more important than today's wants. Try waiting for thirty days (oh all right then, at least seven!) before you buy anything. That should test how strongly you need it.

3 During the period you are waiting, shop around for the best deal you can get. If you are still contemplating using credit remember to compare the APR in the shops you go to, as well as the prices.

4 Don't be afraid to be very un-British – make offers and haggle over prices, especially if you are paying cash. A cash customer is in a much stronger position to bargain than a credit customer.

5 When considering a purchase if you are at all uneasy about the product, the retailer or anything else, don't be afraid to walk out of the shop.

6 Buy items for functional use rather than extras.

7 When you go food shopping do the following:

a Prepare a carefully worked out list before you go, and stick to it. Don't get tempted by 'window shopping', and remember that a 'special offer' is only really special to you if it is something you use regularly anyway.

b Buy supermarket own brands wherever possible. They are nearly always the same quality as the more expensive brands on the shelf beside them.

c Use a calculator to keep a running total as you shop and check it against the till receipt.

d Never go shopping when you are hungry.

e Try not to take your children food shopping. They will almost always put you under pressure and you will end up buying things you didn't intend to.

f Avoid products that are 'out of season' and therefore much more expensive.

g Try to avoid prepared food as much as possible. You are paying for expensive labour and you may well have the time to prepare things yourself.

h Do not buy non-grocery items such as crockery, light bulbs, cassette tapes, etc., in a supermarket unless they are in a sale. They normally have a very high mark-up.

i Fruit and vegetables are almost always cheaper in markets and traditional greengrocers than in supermarkets.

8 Remember that restaurants and fast-food establishments have a very high mark-up.

9 When using your washing machine, oven, dishwasher and so on, try and use them to their maximum potential.

10 Try and buy what you need in end-of-season sales. You can usually get cheap Christmas cards in January or summer clothing in the autumn.

11 Can anyone in your family make Christmas or birthday presents?

12 Can anyone make the family clothing? Is it worth finding an inexpensive way to learn? The same would apply to car maintenance, etc.

13 Can you repair clothing to make it last just a bit longer? Don't throw away items just because a button is missing or a zip has gone.

14 Offer unwanted clothes for sale through dress agencies, which are becoming fashionable. Try buying there too – in certain areas bargains can be had!

15 Can you handle the decoration and maintenance of your home yourself?

16 Keep your financial statement up to date.

17 Keep on looking for ways of maximizing income and minimizing expenditure.

18 Keep a record of what you spend and check against bank statements.

19 Keep receipts and guarantees in case items go wrong.

20 Continue to budget for all irregular bills and expenses, making sure you adjust your financial statement as they occur.

21 Talk to family and friends about how they manage.

22 Help educate your children to manage their own finances as they grow up. You could be saving them much pain and worry in the years ahead.

23 Try and save, even if it is only a little, every month. Your confidence should grow enormously as you see your savings grow, and you realize you have a cushion against any unexpected expenditure.

The more of the above you can do together as a family the easier it will be for you to get clear from debt. As the pressures start to ease so your health and family life should improve and that can only be good news. But do not go to the other extreme and become obsessed with saving. Once you are out of debt it is good to keep unwanted expenses to a minimum, but don't replace the fear of debt with the fear of spending. There is a solution between these two extremes. I hope and pray that you find it.

ACTION PLAN

1 Discover as many ways as possible of saving money appropriate to you and your family situation.
2 Get the whole family involved in coming up with money-saving ideas.

fourteen

And Finally . . . A Summary of Dos and Don'ts

What to do
1 Admit to yourself *all* your debts.
2 Acknowledge that this could affect you and others close to you emotionally.
3 Tell other members of the family straight away.
4 Seek advice when and where necessary.
5 Communicate with all your creditors and keep a copy of all correspondence.
6 Check your benefits position with the DSS immediately.
7 Prepare your financial statement.
8 Separate your priority from your non-priority creditors.
9 Work out what, if anything, can be used to pay off your debts.
10 Make offers to your creditors that are realistic given your budget, and stick to them.

What not to do
1 Put your head in the sand and pretend it isn't happening to you.
2 Fail to tell people close to you what is happening.
3 Refuse to open post and ignore court summonses.
4 Be rude to creditors.
5 Fail to claim benefits.
6 Guess at what you're spending.
7 Buy non-essential items when you still haven't paid for essentials.

8 Make rash promises to pay when you know you are unable to.

9 Cut yourself off from family and friends.

10 Act like Brian . . .

Brian didn't need to know anything about money management. He had a much better way of handling his finances. It was called luck. He nearly always remembered to open the post. When he received a bill he threw it away – he only ever responded to final demands. These he very proudly managed to keep with his bank statements (never looked at) and other correspondence. He kept them where he knew he could find them – behind the clock on the mantelpiece, under the kettle, with the medicine, in his sponge bag.

Most of his money he kept in his current account. He'd used the Miserable Bank for years and didn't care that he got no interest on the account. He thought they looked after him well. About the 22nd of each month they wrote to tell Brian that he had gone overdrawn without permission again. Brian thought it was decent of them to write – so what if he had to pay fees and high interest charges. None the less Brian got a bit cross when the bank manager asked to see him so often. After all, he'd been a customer for a long time.

Brian has had £500 in a Misery Bank deposit account for years. It pays 2% interest. This is his 'rainy day' account but he will not touch it, he likes to have something behind him. His wife had got fed up with his inability to handle his money and had eventually run off with a bailiff. Brian thought they could only take his property with a court summons!

One of Brian's main problems is that he lives on credit. He has 22 credit and store cards, and his main hobby is to juggle money from one to another to ensure he doesn't end up in jail. He had once been warned about being in debt but he hadn't been taught about money, so he just assumed things would eventually sort themselves out. The last thing he was going to do was talk about his situation to anyone else. They might think he was a bit odd.

Brian is not exactly sharp. He has a normal income and has a mortgage — which he hasn't paid for a couple of months because he needed the money for his credit cards. He has also taken out a loan to rent a time-share in Skegness. The loan is secured against his house because it meant the interest was 0.5% lower. But the normally quiet and sober Brian is about to do something outrageous. He has been offered a complete Des O'Connor record collection for £2,000 and tomorrow he is going to buy it with the help of a loan. Rip You Off Limited are only charging 45% interest. This should really change Brian's life . . .

If you think that Brian has any good points please go back to the beginning of the book and read it again more slowly! If not you are on your way to saying goodbye to debt.

Glossary

APR

Annualized Percentage Rate – this includes interest and other charges which the lender may add on.

Benefits Agency

This is where you go to find out about any benefits to which you may be entitled. Until recently it was known as the Department of Social Security (DSS) and is still frequently referred to by these initials.

Default

Failure to maintain payments as previously agreed.

Distraint

Loss of possessions.

Fixed Date Action

The day on which you will be requested to attend court. For example, this could be in regard to house repossession by your mortgage company.

Means-tested

Some benefits are only paid if you have less than a certain amount of capital.

Set Aside Judgement

This is where the court decides to cancel or postpone a previous judgement and usually takes place as a result of a change in your circumstances.

Appendix 1

Summary of Information Needed in a Debt Interview

Family make-up:
Age of children
Number and status of non-dependants
Health of client and family

Housing status:
Relevant details of housing costs, e.g. type of mortgage, amount of payment, etc.
Length of ownership
Approximate equity of house

Details of income:
List of all benefits
Earnings figures including any overtime and all deductions from gross payment, etc.
Non-dependant income
Maintenance
Savings

All relevant expenditure details:
Payment arrangements for the following: Council Tax, Water Rates, Gas, Electricity, Insurance, Car Costs, Telephone

Details on all creditors:
Name and address of Company
Account number
Approximate balance
Type of agreement, i.e. whether a regulated agreement
Details of liability, e.g. husband or wife
Guarantor

Other:
Urgency of action/stage of collection procedure
What action client has already taken
Future prospects

Appendix 2

Benefits Leaflets

Major leaflets available:

1	Which Benefit?	FB2
2	National Insurance Contributions	NP28
3	People on Low Incomes	FB4
4	Income Support	IS1
5	Family Credit	FC1
6	Housing Benefit	RR2
7	Unemployment Benefit	IR41
8	Child Benefit	CH1
9	One-Parent Benefit	CH11
10	Statutory Sick Pay	NI244
11	Disability Living Allowance	DS704
12	Disability Working Allowance	HB4

Leaflets are available from local Benefit Agencies (DSS) or post offices. You can get more help by ringing Freeline Social Security 0800 666555 or, if you are disabled or care for someone with a disability, you can call the Benefit Enquiry Line on 0800 882200.

Leaflets are available in several languages.

Appendix 3

Where to go for help

- Your local Benefits Agency (DSS) for all information on relevant benefits.
- Your local Citizens' Advice Bureau (CAB) or Money Advice Centre – for any advice with regard to budgeting, paying priorities, redundancy entitlements, etc.
- All your (potential) creditors – by negotiating honestly and keeping them up to date you will hopefully be able to make agreements that everyone is happy with.
- Your family and friends – for love, support and encouragement.
- Your doctor – should sickness or depression result.
- Local support groups – where you will be able to give and receive mutual support. Details should be available in Job Centres, libraries, etc.
- Credit Action – 0223-324034 for an overview of money matters, debt and redundancy counselling.
- National Debt Helpline – 021 359 8501.
- Your Local Authority Housing Advice Centre (see telephone directory).
- Shelter (see telephone directory).
  Head Office: 157 Waterloo Road, LONDON SE1 8XF
- Relate (see telephone directory).
- Council of Mortgage Lenders, 3 Savile Row, LONDON W1X 1AF. 071-437 0655.
- Office of Fair Trading, Field House, 15–25 Breams Buildings, LONDON EC4A 1PR. 071-242 2858.
- National Consumer Council, 20 Grosvenor Gardens, LONDON SW1W 0DH. 071-730 3469.
- ACAS (Advisory Conciliation and Arbitration Service), 27 Wilton Street, LONDON SW1X 7AZ. 071-210 3659.